PENGUIN BUSINESS

PIXELS TO PROFITS

Ankur Mehra is a leading authority on the Creator Economy, bringing unique insights from his two decades at the intersection of media platforms, content creators, brands and communities. His diverse background includes senior leadership at Meta, where he led media partnerships for Facebook and Instagram across multiple global regions, including India, Asia-Pacific–Japan, North America and Latin America.

As the former India country manager for Europe's largest YouTube Multi-Channel Network (MCN), he helped shape the digital creator revolution, witnessing first-hand how it transformed the global media landscape. His unconventional perspective is informed by his background as both an EdTech founder and a military veteran.

A LinkedIn 'Top Voice' and respected industry influencer, Ankur shares insights on global MediaTech trends through his weekly newsletter *Creator Economy World*, which reaches C-suite leaders worldwide. He actively shapes the future of digital media through his advisory roles with growth-stage Web 3.0 and MediaTech companies, while mentoring the next generation of entrepreneurs.

This book draws from his extensive experience and offers readers an insider's perspective on navigating and succeeding in the rapidly evolving Creator Economy.

ADVANCE PRAISE FOR THE BOOK

'The Creator Economy isn't just a buzzword; it is the present and future of how we work, connect and grow. Discover the stories, trends and strategies behind this revolution and how it can inspire your journey'—**Ankur Warikoo, entrepreneur and writer**

'This book is an invaluable resource that demystifies the Creator Economy while highlighting its boundless opportunities. A must-read for anyone seeking to understand the future of digital expression and entrepreneurship'—**Shalini Passi, art patron and media personality**

'A very important book. The Creator Economy is here to stay'—**Anshula Kapoor, writer and public speaker**

Pixels to Profits

A Systematic Deep Dive into the Creator Economy

ANKUR MEHRA

**PENGUIN
BUSINESS**

An imprint of Penguin Random House

PENGUIN BUSINESS

Penguin Business is an imprint of the Penguin Random House group of
companies whose addresses can be found at global.penguinrandomhouse.com

Published by Penguin Random House India Pvt. Ltd
4th Floor, Capital Tower 1, MG Road,
Gurugram 122 002, Haryana, India

First published in Penguin Business by Penguin Random House India 2025

ISBN 9780143472964

Typeset in Garamond by MAP Systems, Bengaluru, India
Printed at Thomson Press India Ltd, New Delhi

www.penguin.co.in

Contents

Foreword

When social media platforms started booming in the mid-2000s, it opened up a whole new world for all of us. We could see pictures our friends had just clicked, connect with anyone across the globe and even share our videos online.

As commonplace as it may sound today, it was nothing short of being miraculous back then.

Two decades later, as of date, social media platforms have not only magnified the quantum of things they can do, but they have also gone on to create an entire ecosystem, called the Creator Economy. As a result, the way consumers interact with their products and how businesses sell them has undergone a transformation.

The Creator Economy is estimated to be valued at a staggering half a trillion dollars by 2027.[1]

The traditional cycle of a customer discovering a product through TV, magazines or newspaper advertisements and purchasing it from a nearby mom-and-pop store or a supermarket has also changed. Likewise, the way trust is built between the business and the customer has also shifted.

Now we are not just sharing our personal life updates with our friends and family online. We are also making purchases after looking at content that resonates with our needs and wants. We consume content as naturally as we consume food.

On the other hand, a lot of us are also creating content as full-time/part-time employment. In parallel, businesses are working with these content creators to drive awareness and sales—a concept they were never taught in their B-school education.

Organizations have designated teams working on different social media platforms, responsible for driving numbers. Not only that, but unique solutions are also being created to support and fuel the growth of this new industry.

However, the one thing that has remained constant is that the consumer is still the deciding factor in the ecosystem.

Thus, I believe a book detailing the depths of this evolving equation between the consumer and the creator is the need of the hour.

It will help businesses have a better understanding of how to make the best use of the creator marketplace to reach their end consumers.

Creators will understand the nuances of how best to make use of their talent to reach existing and new audiences while monetizing their efforts at different points of this journey. This book will also provide much-needed inspiration for creators sitting on the fence to take the leap and start with content creation.

There are key takeaways for everyone who is a part of the Creator Economy—whether it is creators, traditional businesses (that are now building an online presence after decades of offline existence), social media channels, digital businesses that thrive on the Creator Economy, or the consumer, who is the backbone of every business.

Ankur, with nearly two decades navigating the dynamic media landscape, brings a wealth of experience to this book. With a remarkable journey managing over 1,20,000 creators across YouTube, Instagram and Facebook, coupled with an extensive global tenure at Meta—from the Silicon Valley to the bustling Indian markets—Ankur has meticulously deconstructed the intricacies of the Creator Economy in a manner that is both comprehensive and accessible.

His trajectory from serving as a major in the Indian Army to achieving groundbreaking milestones in the media industry, including founding a successful venture with a noteworthy exit, is an example of his relentless commitment to being a student of innovation and excellence.

Through this book, Ankur invites you to explore the Creator Economy with a realistic approach. His use of simple, everyday words offers actionable insights to the reader. Whether you're an executive, an entrepreneur or an aspiring creator in the Creator Economy, this book will guide your steps.

The world is rapidly evolving with digital innovation and creative expression being the catalysts. As we learn to find our way in this new normal, we must embrace the opportunities that lie before us. After all, in the world in which we live, the customer is the king and the screen is the queen.

To you, the reader, I extend my best wishes as you embark on this journey. And to Ankur, I commend you for undertaking the vital task of documenting the Creator Economy's evolution.

Keki B. Dadiseth
Former chairman, Sony India, former chairman, Hindustan Unilever Ltd and board member, non-executive adviser to Marsh McLennan, The Indian Hotels Co. Ltd and the Indian School of Business, among others

Preface

Why do you need a book on the Creator Economy?

What is it that I have to offer you that would change anything in your life as a creator?

Why can't you just start recording videos or podcasts or write your thoughts and 'wait' to be discovered—quit your boring job and turn content-creation into your full-time business?

Why should you listen to me?

Don't.

But I think experience is the loudest even when education and evangelization have lost their voice. I'm very grateful for the fact that I have closely witnessed the evolution of the Creator Economy for more than fifteen years. From working with traditional broadcasters that offered a few channels to now where we have infinite media and channels in our very hands.

In that journey, I have been able to gather experience, and understanding of the nitty-gritties of how the Creator Economy functions.

From working with creators from all walks of life, from Hyderabad to San Francisco, from Rajinikanth to Nas Daily, and from being an insider in the digital media industry since its inception to watching it take over the world—my journey has truly been the best of both worlds. These deep learnings, I believe, are for everyone to benefit from, even if you haven't ever been remotely related to the Creator Economy or any of its branches.

From where I can see, I have been a learner and a silent spectator. And now, maybe no more silent, an author or a voice in the Creator Economy.

Don't get me wrong. I'm no guru. I'm not the creator of the Creator Economy.

This book is my humble attempt to share what I have been blessed to know about the Creator Economy—a resource that aims to help all its moving parts: creators, brands, consumers, platforms and the businesses that are built out of these.

It's not that I know everything, but I am a big believer in understanding and execution, rather than just accumulating knowledge with zero action. This is what gives our conversation an edge and makes spending time together worthwhile.

Thus, the journey of this book, laid out in simple yet practical ways, will help many of you to:

- Understand the nuances of how to monetize your creativity as a creator or build a brand in the Creator Economy
- Build a business around and out of content creation

This isn't just a book to 'work for a new hobby'. This book will help you create a revolutionary parallel economy for yourself through a viable, time-tested and practical business model.

Which brings me to an idea of a revolution.

We often think and speak about 'revolutionary business ideas'. However, the truth about a revolution is you don't wake up one day and have one. It happens one tiny change at a time and one day at a time that is visibly insignificant in the bigger scheme of things.

Put those closely related tiny things together for long enough, and you have a revolution. A revolution is often an outcome of an evolution.

The Creator Economy is exactly that revolution. It didn't happen overnight. It has been growing and evolving for more than a century, and I am not surprised by how it has unfolded.

From tiny evolutions, tracing its history from the first motion pictures in the late nineteenth century to the rise of platforms like YouTube and social media in the 2000s, it has truly become a revolution.

The growth of social media, and consequently the Creator Economy, accelerated during the COVID-19 pandemic, with over 165 million new creators joining since 2020 (as per a 2023 study by Adobe).[1]

While the term 'Creator Economy' is being used very liberally these days, there is a lack of literature on the subject and even less understanding of it among the general populace. The purpose of this book is to bring out a ringside view of this up-and-coming industry from the point of view of someone who has worked with more than 1,20,000 creators across platforms such as YouTube, Facebook and Instagram, and seen the inner workings of the media and marketing worlds.

Without taking much of your time, here is something I want to leave you with:

People don't become professional weightlifters by lifting weights in their local gym three times a week.

Roger Federer did not become Roger Federer by playing tennis in his apartment complex tennis court, three times a week.

Jony Ive, the master designer and Steve Jobs's right hand, who designed revolutionary products at Apple, did not just get there by taking up a ten-day online course on designing.

There were years, perhaps decades of hard work, relentless learning of what excellence in their craft required, and then finally cracking the game.

This book does exactly that—for your journey to winning in the Creator Economy.

I have spent several years and decades learning so you get the recipe in your hands without having to spend that time yourself.

As a fence-sitter or an early adapter, I believe you can participate in the Creator Economy by one of the two ways:

1. Your skills and comfort
2. Your understanding of the playing field

This book aims for the latter, ensuring the playing field is levelled for every single one of you reading it.

This book is my attempt to simplify, deconstruct and democratize the concept of media and the creator space.

Whether you are an individual creator, a small brand or a budding innovator in the tech space, or someone dabbling with the thought of whether the Creator Economy is for you—and if it is, how to thrive in it—this book attempts to provide the answers you are looking for. Probably much more.

The 5C Framework of the Creator Economy

When you talk about a book on the Creator Economy, the default assumption is often that it's about becoming a creator—start to share your pictures, music, writing, videos, podcast, code and more with the world, all the while believing you will be successful.

While that is true, it is only one pillar of the truth.

When the creator creates content, which channel or platform do they create content on?

When the creator creates content on a channel, they end up building a community of consumers that absorb their content.

When the creator builds a community by producing content for a channel, they attract collaborators and business partners—brands that offer them opportunities to promote their products. The brand gains visibility, sales and more, while the creator gets paid by the collaborators.

However, there are a multitude of other ways a creator can make money in the Creator Economy—over and above brand deals—through sponsorships, affiliate marketing, selling merchandise, building courses and many more. This is how you create commerce in the Creator Economy.

All of these five pillars—creators, channels, collaborators, commerce and consumers—drive the Creator Economy together, growing stronger and estimated to reach half a trillion dollars by 2027.[1]

Through the pages of this book, we will talk about how the Creator Economy started in the first place, how content creation got global, how the availability of content for all sparked a revolution, which led to 'content creation' becoming a full-time economy, and what the future holds for us.

Thus, before we step in and understand the concept inside out, here is a brief conversation on all the five pillars that drive it. We will speak about these in detail across Chapters 3, 4 and 5. However, to set the ground for you, here they are:

1. Creators

Creators are the soul, the essence of the Creator Economy. They are the ones who create content and build communities from scratch. They set trends, make things exciting for all of us to witness and help the economy flourish.

2. Channels

These are popular platforms such as YouTube, Instagram, TikTok, Facebook, LinkedIn, Instagram Threads, Airchat, Pinterest, X and other niche sites where creators produce their content. These are the stages where creators perform, helping to build a solid foundation that keeps the Creator Economy going.

3. Community/Consumers

As consumers, we might think we are only consuming what creators and channels serve us. However, our actions— liking, commenting, sharing and subscribing—actively shape the content creators produce, influencing algorithms and driving trends.

We have more power than we think.

4. Collaborators

Businesses aim to attract more attention to their products when they are actively engaging in the Creator Economy. Thus, creators with a dedicated audience not only attract businesses to collaborate with them but also help drive revenue or build awareness around their products.

5. Commerce

In addition to working with collaborators, creators find other ways of generating revenue streams, such as speaking engagements, affiliate marketing, selling merchandise, becoming instructors or collaborator brand channels, launching their own courses, writing books or even creating their own product lines—the possibilities are endless.

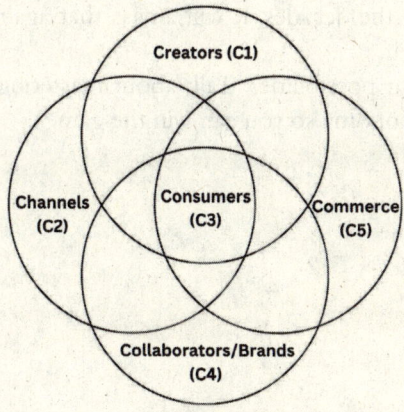

**The 5Cs of the
Creator Economy**

However, it is prudent to know that success in every business is a game of statistics, and the Creator Economy is no different.

In this book, we will explore the journeys of multiple creators and see how they made it big in the Creator Economy. However, I would also like to point out that not everyone who sets out to create content makes it big. Sometimes, it is not prudent to quit your job and go all in.

My job in this book is to show you the vibrant, thriving and business side of the Creator Economy. However, it is not an instruction manual to quitting your job and diving headfirst into a full-time career in content creation.

I want to stay true to you as much as possible, and that is why you must discard any insight or advice that offers you 100 per cent guaranteed results.

But, as I put you to read data, I must also tell you that more than 165 million (16.5 crore) creators have joined the Creator Economy since 2020. It is projected to grow from $250 billion in 2023 to $480 billion by 2027, nearly doubling in size.

The size that the current state of the Creator Economy has amassed over the decades, it will amass that again in the next four years itself.

Talk about possibilities. Talk about mastering the ins and outs of the economy so you can win the game.

Influencer or Creator?

Who is a creator and who is an influencer?

Are they different?

If they are, how should you differentiate the two words throughout the book?

If we go by their technical definitions, a creator and an influencer are two different people who merge at one small arc—to become creators who exert influence.

However, my role in this book is to make things clear for you, not complex. Thus, throughout the book, we will use the words creator and influencer interchangeably, as they are in common parlance.

If you are a nerd, you can skip to the detailed, defined and refined definition and differentiation of creator and influencer in Chapter 3(d). However, for the rest of the book and to keep things simple and easy to understand, we use these words in place of each other.

Let's keep complexity outside the door and enter the exciting world of the Creator Economy.

Chapter 1

The First and the Foremost

'Shift the antenna a little bit left, a bit to the right. A little more right. A bit more.'

'There you go!'

Growing up in the 1980s in India, the biggest source of entertainment for us was television.

When I say *us,* it means my sister, my parents and I. And millions of other households at the time.

Entertainment used to be a family exercise, not the democratized experience we have today with personalized subscriptions and screens in every room.

The television sets were also peculiar, to say the least. There were no 4K, flat-screen, 3D experiences, larger than life TVs that we have in our living rooms these days. It was something like a big box with a protruding belly-shaped screen, used by the entire family.

The TV operated by receiving signals from the antenna which was installed at the terrace of every house. My parents would often have conversations about signal reception and disturbance when the TV inside our house stopped functioning.

This would lead my father to the terrace to fix the antenna (read: move it a bit till we got the signal in the TV downstairs) with my mom giving him instructions till the reception was clear.

We made do with one TV for the entire family, taking turns to manually change channels. (Yes, we had to walk up to the set to change them).

When the more advanced television sets took over our living rooms, we would fight for control over the remote.

'Dude, why didn't you just watch your content on your phone?'

Fun fact: Back then, we didn't call it 'content'. It was simply known as a 'serial'—a term that might sound almost alien in today's 'content' world.

Because dude, this was the decade of the 1980s and 1990s, and the concept of mobile phones wasn't relatively new, it was non-existent.

Anyway, coming back to the box or CRT TV sets, my earliest memories of watching content involve my father going up to the terrace to adjust the antenna.

As I reached my early teens, I took the baton from my dad and became the one my family would entrust to go to the terrace and fix the antenna. It was perhaps my adolescent equivalent of getting a glass with more milkshake than the one my sister had.

Fun fact: Those TV sets would have no more than eight to ten channels. My optimistic memory makes me believe it was no more than eight, but if someone from my era wants to slap the facts to my face, to tell me it was even less, I am sure you are right.

Even with such limited content to consume, we still had weekly curfews on TV time, especially as we waited in anticipation to watch the Sunday broadcasts of Mahabharat and Ramayana.

Anyway, life happened, we grew, and so did our avenues of content. The antenna era was followed by the cable television era, bringing a plethora of channels to explore.

We had weekly shows like *Antakshari* and *Hum Paanch*, to name a few. It was also around this time that we got our first taste of international shows.

From *Small Wonder* with Vicki the Robot to the thrill of Disney Hour on Sunday mornings and the action-packed drama of *Baywatch*, the cable television era truly spoiled us for choice.

My personal favorites were *The Wonder Years* and *I Dream of Jeannie*. My sister loved watching *Beverly Hills 90210*, and the entire family huddled when *M.A.S.H.* aired. Yes, those were the single screen and single remote-control days.

The third phase of content viewership came when the cable TV was replaced by the dish antenna, or more popularly known as DTH (Direct to Home) service. With players like Dish TV and Airtel TV and Tata Sky (now Tata Play), every big player roped in one or an other mega star of Indian cinema, ranging from Shah Rukh Khan to Aamir Khan, as their brand ambassadors.

At the same time, digitalization was taking place on our other screens, computers and the internet was becoming accessible to everyone. This was also the time of Yahoo Chat Rooms (sorry Gen Z!). It was a way of connecting with strangers online beyond pen pals.

Okay, breathe.

I'll explain.

As a kid, we could make friends with strangers through the International Pen Friends Association. We could write letters and also receive some, in turn. It was a wholesome *validation* and dopamine, thankfully delivered without the fleeting attention span of a goldfish. Those friends, also called pen pals, were my, and I believe for a lot of people, first introduction to international strangers.

As a grown up, it was replaced by the Yahoo Messenger.

Think of WhatsApp in today's era. But with strangers. On a desktop, instead of a cell phone.

ASL (Age-Sex-Location) was the ice-breaking conversation we would ask a random stranger. With this information, you would decide if you wanted to take the conversation any further or not. It was a mandatory rite-of-passage question whenever you entered a chat room. Also, one could 'BUZZ' the other side on a private chat that would 'shake up' the chat window for attention. Yeah, we were weird. But tell me one generation that isn't.

Anyway, what these pen pals and messenger friends did was foster bonds, create opportunities for culture exchange, built trust and facilitate the formation of new connections. Of course, not all such friendships—indeed, most of them—morphed into meaningful ones. However, it was a powerful deep dive into our core human need for connection.

Years later, today, you and I can connect with any stranger in any corner of the world.

Through what the Creator Economy has enabled, we can also scroll through someone's content over the years and instantly decide if we want to be friends with them, follow them, or maybe want to keep them away from our circle of online influence.

These creators earn our trust and connect with us on a deeper level, tapping into our universal need for connection.

Chapter 1(a)

Beginning of the Videos

'I am experimenting upon an instrument which does for the Eye what the phonograph does for the Ear, which is the recording and reproduction of things in motion,' wrote Thomas Edison in 1888 while filing a patent for a video-producing device.

Most of us know Thomas Edison as the inventor of the light bulb. However, he is also a distant inventor of the light on our blue screen.

Turns out, the first prototype of a motion picture was a kinetoscope that enabled us to view moving pictures, one at a time. It was demonstrated in 1891 by the Edison Company, and the first public demonstration took place in 1893. By 1894, the kinetoscope was already a commercial success.

Talk about going viral more than a century ago!

However, motion pictures were first invented in Paris, France, in 1895 by Auguste and Louis Lumière, famously known as the Lumière brothers. Antoine Lumière, their father, who had a photographic business, saw a kinetoscope in Paris and encouraged his sons to devise an apparatus that would capture and project moving pictures.

The first device was called cinématographe. As it was remarkably compact, it could be taken anywhere, either to shoot a film or to use as a projector. Surprisingly, it did not rely on electric power unlike the Edison Company's kinetoscope.

Zooming out for a moment, isn't it surreal that even over a century ago, devices existed to shoot films. Think about it—creators existed long before the Creator Economy came into being.

Anyway, Antoine decided to launch the device publicly on 28 December 1895. He ran multiple shows featuring ten films, each lasting fifteen minutes. And on some days, he made money amounting to 2,500 francs (more than £42,000 as of 2024).

Over the next 111 years, motion pictures embarked on an extraordinary journey, evolving through animations, colour films, sound films, broadcast TV shows, film-based TV shows, TV commercial ads, virtual reality, taped TV shows, music videos, DVDs and web series.

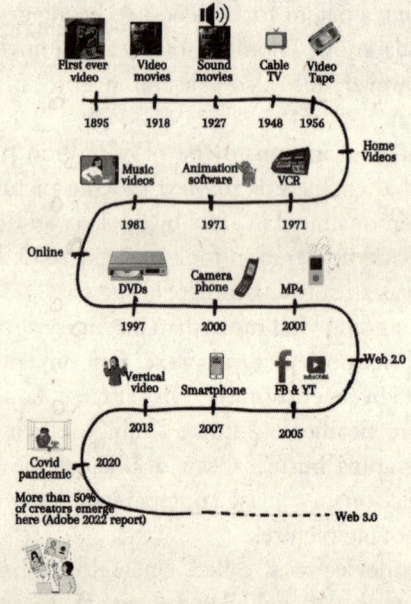

A journey of evolution of content over more than a century

The way videos are being consumed by every generation and every individual—regardless of profession or location—is truly mind-boggling.

From *Baby Shark* and *Peppa Pig* introducing education to toddlers, to boomers consuming sermons and devotional songs, videos have become as essential as oxygen. Everyone consumes them.

That is why I want to ask you a weird question.

Think about the last time you went an entire month without watching any videos.

A week? Or maybe just 24 hours? It is almost impossible to remember when that last happened, isn't it?

Now, think of your parents' generation. How many videos did they watch on a daily basis back in the day? My parents didn't even have a wedding video. Videos simply weren't a thing back then.

In a world where the smartest minds are constantly working to keep you engaged on their video platforms for as long as possible, it is hard to imagine a time when a world without videos even existed.

But it did.

In all its sanity and sanctity.

In all its peace and privacy.

In all its freedom and fierceness.

For a long time, the devices in our hands have been the primary source from which we consume videos. Prior to that, consuming videos on our laptops or personal computers was considered cool. A few years before that, television sets were the rockstars (and still are, in their modern forms). Prior to colour television sets, there were black and white television sets.

Before television sets, radio was the dominant form of media for the longest time. I would also like to believe the radio was one of the most impactful forms of communication in the pre-internet era.

Here are some fun facts about radio that you'd love:

Fun fact #1: In the early 1890s, Marconi started working on the idea of 'wireless telegraphy'. By the start of the next decade, in 1909, he went on to win the Nobel Prize with Karl Ferdinand Braun for their 'contributions to the development of wireless telegraphy' (radio communications).

So, I may not be wrong if we say that the modern-day television and internet emerged from the contributions of Marconi, Edison and Lumière brothers combined. Talk about evolution resulting in a revolution.

Fun fact #2: After the sinking of the RMS Titanic on 15 April 1912, the surviving passengers were rescued by a transatlantic passenger steamship Carpathia, which took seventeen minutes to receive and decode the SOS signal sent by the ship. After this incident, Marconi gained popularity and became more recognized for his contributions to the field of radio and wireless technology. On 18 June 1912 Marconi testified before the Court of Inquiry into the loss of the Titanic, explaining the functions of marine telegraphy and the procedures for emergencies at sea. Britain's Postmaster-General summed up the Titanic disaster, stating: 'Those who have been saved, have been saved through one man, Mr. Marconi . . . and his marvellous invention.'

But what else led to the evolution and revolution from radio to television?

I would like to believe that in the world of media (and now devices), a new product or invention is always on the cusp.

It is not a matter of 'if'; it is a matter of 'when'.

Radio became popular in the years before World War I. It was mostly used for maritime and aircraft navigation. However, during World War II, it became the most popular medium for spreading propaganda news, advertisement and entertainment, including music and drama.

Today, we consume all our media on digital devices. But did such devices exist during the World Wars?

They did—though in the form of larger, single-function devices called transistors, designed to receive signals from various channels and transmit them to receivers.

It was only after World War II that television rapidly replaced radio as the new mass medium. What started with experimental broadcast stations in the 1930s eventually replaced the radio as the most dominant broadcast medium by the 1950s.

It turns out, in 1946, approximately 8,000 US households had television sets. By 1960, 45.7 million households had them.[1]

The decades that followed led to multiple transformations of the television, such as:

- Bulky black and white television sets, where you had to turn the knob around to change channels.
- Colour television sets, now operable with battery-powered remote controls.
- Flat television sets with remote controls.

Through all these stages of evolution, the mode of 'receiving signals' remained a wired antenna, carefully positioned at a specific angle on the terrace to broadcast TV channels.

It was followed by umbrella-style dish antennas, which are still prevalent today to some extent.

With social media taking over the world in the mid-2000s, the TV industry witnessed its next revolution with OTT (over-the-top) platforms streaming digital content through internet-connected devices, including phones, iPads, computers, laptops and even televisions.

So, from Marconi winning the Nobel Prize in Physics in 1909 to the internet revolution in the early 2000s, it took almost a century for TV to become mainstream and also lose its power to devices.

Over the past two decades, the internet has evolved from being a tool for searching for important information on Google and checking who viewed your social media profiles to becoming our primary source of consumption, education, companionship, employment, and endless discoveries, shaping our lives day in and day out.

Key takeaways:

- It took more than a century for videos to be 'invented' and then to become mainstream and reach the masses.
- It took almost a tenth of that number (ten years) for social media to become mainstream, reach the masses and even create an economy. Fun fact: It took ChatGPT five days to reach one million users, whereas the Threads App by Meta took just an hour to get to one million users!
- Compounding is not a phenomenon of the stock market only. It is a phenomenon of life. And of course, the Creator Economy.

Chapter 1(b)

From Idiot Box to Smartphones

'Television won't be able to hold on to any market it captures after the first six months. People will soon get tired of staring at a plywood box every night'

—Darryl F. Zanuck of
20th Century Fox, in 1946[2]

20 July 1969 is a landmark event in the history of the world.

On this day, Neil Armstrong became the first man to land on the moon, fulfilling President Kennedy's vision of landing a human on the lunar surface by the end of the 1960s and safely bringing them back to Earth.

Not only this, a whopping 650 million people watched the live telecast of the event. In the United States alone, 93 per cent of televisions tuned in to see Armstrong walk on the moon.[3]

Wait, what—wasn't radio the most popular means of communication until the second World War?

It indeed was. However, after World War II, television broadcasting became an important mass medium for advertising and entertainment. By 1960, 90 per cent of America had a television.

In 1961, President Kennedy gave his first live televised press conference. Television, however, truly went global in 1962 with the launch of the communication satellite Telstar I.

Over the next three decades, TV gained widespread acceptance worldwide, covering everything from news, sports broadcasts, and political events to television interviews, Super Bowls, and sitcoms.

In fact, when Neil Armstrong's first moonwalk was broadcast live in 1969, it offered an early glimpse of global connectivity—an experience akin to online communities, long before the internet was invented. Just that, we did not know it was an online community.

The 1970s and 1980s saw a significant rise in TV viewership, with shows becoming increasingly popular, along with the introduction of commercial breaks. This also gave way to water cooler shows, especially the ones that became hugely popular, including *Seinfeld* and *Friends*.

The shows connected to the core human emotions of humour, being flawed, being work-in-progress, yet having fun, and thus, leading to bonding of people (read: communities).

The popularity of TV shows like *Friends*, *Seinfeld* and *Dallas* sparked the production of hundreds of similar shows worldwide. Little did we know that, just beyond the millennium, Web 2.0 was waiting to transform our digital experience.

...

In another revolution unfolding on a different screen within the same home, the first social network, Six Degrees, was launched in 1997. It offered everything a social profile could be—allowing users to create their own profile, maintain a list of friends and interact with them through private messages.

It was built on the concept of Six Degrees of Separation, meaning every person is connected to any other person in the world through six intermediaries, and anyone could join. People who confirmed relationships with other users but did not register their profiles with the site continued to receive occasional emails, perhaps an indirect nudge to hop on.

As a matter of fact, the social network gathered more than 3.5 million users in the next three years. However, because it failed to monetize, it was eaten up by the bubble burst of the year 2000.

This was followed by other social media sites such as Blogger (for posting blogs) in 1999, Friendster in 2001, LinkedIn in 2002 and MySpace in 2003.

Contrary to popular belief, LinkedIn was launched long before Facebook, although its user growth peaked well after Facebook (and its subsidiary Instagram) had reached theirs.

Almost all of these social media sites tanked in a few years, except for LinkedIn, Facebook, Instagram and a few others. However, the collapse was merely the dismantling of old structures, paving the way for the emergence of newer, stronger ones.

Key takeaways:

- Modern day 'content creation' began as TV shows and movies, especially sitcoms, that related to mass appeal.
- It laid the foundation for social media to take off in the first and second decades of the next millennium.
- The rise and fall of social media platforms is something many people of that era witnessed and continue to witness. Volatility has become the second nature of the internet industry.

Chapter 1(c)

Say Hello to Social Media

Then came the years 2005 and 2006.

In 2005 and 2006, two major developments reshaped the way the world viewed videos:

1. YouTube
2. Facebook.

Let us dissect each of them as to why they are significant landmarks in the evolution of social media.

YouTube was launched on 14 February 2005.

The founders Chad Hurley, Steve Chen and Jawed Karim wanted to make it simple for people to publish and distribute videos globally. What is helpful to note is that YouTube has eventually gone on to become a communication platform that enables building communities, going beyond being just a destination for publishing videos.

It is an enabler, rather than just a storage platform.

The first ever YouTube video of 'Me at the Zoo' was uploaded on Jawed Karim's channel on 24 April 2005. To date (early 2025), it has garnered more than 345 million views.

It's surprising that the founder of YouTube is not a creator on the platform, yet still has a following of 4.87 million subscribers.

While the three founders of YouTube had unknowingly started a revolution in Menlo Park, California, another (would-be) revolutionary, Mark Zuckerberg, was bringing forth the origin of Web 2.0, three miles away in Palo Alto, California.[4]

Facebook started in 2004 as a social networking site exclusively for Harvard students. Over time, it gradually became the go-to platform for social networking—sharing photos and status updates with friends—and launched its video feature in 2006.

A remarkable landmark in Facebook's journey as the leader of the Creator Economy came in 2012 when it acquired the less-than-two-year-old photo sharing platform Instagram in 2012, for $1 billion. As of 2023, Instagram has gone on to generate $49.8 billion in revenue, which accounts for 37 per cent of Facebook's total revenue.[5]

Why Did Facebook and YouTube thrive, and Others Didn't?

Facebook was not the first social networking site. Two very popular social networking sites that existed before Facebook were MySpace and Orkut.

As a matter of fact, from 2005-2009, MySpace was the largest social networking site in the world. It also saw various landmark achievements, such as:

- It surpassed Yahoo! and Google to become the most visited site in the US, in the year 2006.
- Generated revenues of $800 million during the 2008 fiscal year (Facebook was a loss-making entity in 2008).

However, in April 2008, Facebook quickly surpassed MySpace in terms of global users. And a year later in May 2009, it again surpassed MySpace in number of unique US visitors. After years of declining valuation and visitors, MySpace had dropped to 7 million monthly visitors by 2019, down from 115 million in 2008. On the other hand, Facebook went on to become profitable for the first time in 2009—and remained so every year thereafter.

It is believed that MySpace stuck to a 'portal strategy'. Its focus was to build an audience around entertainment and music. Facebook, on the other hand, pivoted itself to a mobile-first strategy, adding new features to enhance the social networking experience. This constant enhancement of features kept users hooked on Facebook and Twitter (now X), which likely contributed to MySpace's decline.

With the launch of iPhone in 2007 and iPod features almost migrating there seamlessly, it also held a smaller ground for MySpace to create its dominance. It was probably at the right place but at the wrong time, perhaps late by several years.

The reason Orkut couldn't keep up with Facebook was that its servers couldn't handle the rapidly increasing number of users, resulting in slower loading times. The low internet speeds of the time further compounded the hassle.

Also, the success of a product in any market is defined by its execution to make things simpler for its users. Orkut failed to keep the fundamental promise of simplifying the user experience, unlike Facebook, where viewing notifications, messages and friends was very simple, consistently updated, and the red 'notification' number prompted users to linger longer.

Another important feature of Facebook was that no one could see who viewed their profile, whereas Orkut clearly displayed this information. While it gave a dopamine hit to the user, it also meant not being able to 'stalk' people without them being aware, which, let's admit it, is a feature most of us want on social media.

Along with social media sites, I must mention the portal websites of MSN, Yahoo! and Google.

Google went public in 2004 and acquired YouTube in late 2006. Though Google's in-house social media networks of

Orkut and Google+ could not create a revolution, Google's innovations as a search engine giant, and now a tech giant, have always kept it in the forefront.

When we speak of MSN and Yahoo!, these were the two most visited sites in the United States in 2005, when Facebook and YouTube had just started.

However, over the years, MSN underwent constant rebranding and reshuffling of its core features, while Google continued to rise as the most popular search engine.

One of Yahoo!'s most significant missteps was its decision to forgo acquiring Google. Not once, but twice. In 1998 Google offered to be acquired by Yahoo! for just $1 million. In 2002 again, the tech giant offered to be acquired for $5 billion.

In hindsight, what seemed like a crisis for Google became its biggest opportunity ever. In 2004, when Google went public, its co-founders Larry Page, Sergey Brin and Eric Schmidt agreed to work together at the company for twenty years, until 2024. At Yahoo!, the leadership crisis was a major issue, with the return of its co-founder Jerry Yang as CEO, followed by subsequent CEOs Carol Bartz, Scott Thompson and Marissa Mayer, who also couldn't bring the company back to its original magic.

From being a company nearly acquired twice within its first five years, Google (now Alphabet) has risen to become one of the five most valuable companies in the world.

With Facebook, more people were getting connected online, leading to an array of revolutions in the years after—chats, video chats, iPhone and other smartphones, followed by every social networking platform embracing videos.

Because Facebook allowed people to 'see' each other's faces, it also accelerated the growth of communities, which were almost non-existent, or in traces, on platforms before.

To put my understanding of the Creator Economy, I believe YouTube and Facebook thrived because they gave the users infinite access to videos. With Instagram contributing to 37 per cent of the latter's revenue, it remains a cash cow for the company while continuing to captivate the attention of Gen Alpha, Gen Z and millennials.

The Social Media Spin-Off into Communities

Little did we know through the growth of social media that we were now creating an ecosystem that would not only create a lot of jobs virtually through the power of communities but also bring offline jobs online.

Zomato, the Indian multinational restaurant aggregator and food delivery company, does a fantastic job at this. If you go through the brand's social media handles, it does not advertise its food delivery services, restaurant partners or any of the app updates. They prefer focusing on memes and other engaging content.

They create food memes, using self-deprecating humour, frequently challenge norms, jump on moment marketing trends, and have even enlisted top comedians to roast them on their anniversary. Their notifications are case studies that are quoted in almost all marketing rooms in closed doors.

They've cracked the code by understanding what their audience truly stands for. So, instead of asking them to 'order food, save time', they speak the audience's language: of fun.

Founder Deepinder Goyal also gets on a chat with top chefs across the country and publishes them on the Zomato YouTube channel, which, I believe, is a good peep into the BTS (behind the scenes) of how the restaurant industry operates, for laymen like you and I, who know less about the industry and yet love our food.

In my conversations with friends about marketing strategies, I often come across examples of how companies with offline products have brilliantly leveraged online marketing. They've shown how even offline-only brands can harness the power of an online presence to connect with their audience effectively.

If we zoom out on that for a bit, Zomato has a huge communications team that includes content creators, video editors, designers, creative writers, marketers, and several other roles that you and I are perhaps not aware of—that virtually drive every communication of the brand online.

While it may seem obvious, social media has created a plethora of opportunities across nearly every industry. Even mentioning it is an understatement since most companies have an essential social media department just like they have an HR department.

While Zomato has done an excellent job of bringing an offline-only business online in a spectacular way, Airbnb has done the reverse. Airbnb, the company that offers homestays for travellers by acting as a broker between the property owners and the customers, has a popular arm of its experiences—'Airbnb Experiences'.

Airbnb Experiences offer unique, immersive activities that allow travellers to explore their destination through the eyes of a local. These are not just local tours with a tour guide, these are immersive experiences that not just show travellers where to stay, but also what to do.

With the slogan of 'live like a local', Airbnb Experiences are niche tours that allow travellers to enjoy their hobbies and interests in a fresh and culturally immersive way.

The best part, you ask. Tour guides and activity operators don't need to host homes on Airbnb to host an experience. And travellers don't need to stay in an Airbnb home to participate in an Airbnb Experience. Airbnb Experiences is open to all.

It is a completely different service from Airbnb hosting. Hosts don't need to have overnight guests in their homes to participate in the Airbnb experience, unless the experience calls for it.

The Creator Economy has not only made us more social, but it has also made us connect with our uniqueness—be it watching memes by a public company or going on a tour of your own city or the city you are travelling to.

What is the opposite of the Creator Economy? Borders and restrictions.

Key takeaways:

- YouTube and Facebook served as rocket fuel in the creation of community-based platforms.
- While they have managed to survive the death of a lot of their co-existing social media platforms, they have led to the creation of the bustling Creator Economy and the power they hold.

Chapter 1(d)

Viral Video Trends

Imagine being just twenty-six-years old and having your music video as the second most-viewed video on YouTube and the second most-streamed song on Spotify.

In January 2025, 'Shape of You' stands as the seventh most viewed video on YouTube with approximately 6.39 billion views. 'The best songs that I've ever written, I don't really remember writing,' Ed Sheeran confessed.[6] 'They take like 20 minutes and then they're just done. And then you move on to the next thing,' he added.

As a matter of fact, Sheeran did not write the 'Shape of You' song to be his best song. It was written during a brainstorming session in a studio, alongside his longtime friend, Johnny McDaid. However, only after the song was composed, someone from his team suggested that Sheeran should go about using it.

Sometimes, ignoring your own self-doubts and listening to those in your circle can change your entire life.

That is the case with virality.

You do not know what is going to happen, when the next viral sensation is going to disrupt the world, and when a brand is going to jump on the bandwagon and make that storytelling the talk of the town. However, I would like to step back and discuss what virality really us.

Wikipedia defines 'viral video' as a video that becomes popular through a viral process of internet sharing, typically through video sharing websites such as YouTube, as well as social media and email.

Just as viruses spread in humans, the term 'viral', when applied to a digital asset, refers to content that rapidly spreads to a large number of online users in a short period.

There is no 'set criteria' for a video or a piece of content to go viral. However, when the piece of content reaches an exponentially larger audience compared to others, it is referred to as viral content. Research suggests the following to be pushing factors to make a viral video:

- The hook, often a memorable phrase or moment, can become a part of the viral video culture after being shown repeatedly. Hooks, or key signifiers, cannot be predicted before a video goes viral.
- Another study at the University of Texas at Dallas found that people preferred to share a funny video rather than an educational or insightful video. Overall, they were more likely to share any video that evoked an intense emotional response.
- Two professors at the Wharton School at the University of Pennsylvania also found that uplifting stories were more likely to be shared on the New York Times' website than disheartening ones.

From a purely financial perspective, the more a video is played on YouTube or on X, or any other social platform, the more its creator becomes eligible for higher revenue.

By 2014, pop stars such as Justin Bieber, Miley Cyrus, Eminem and Katy Perry were consistently attracting web traffic in the range of 120 to 150 million hits per month; numbers far in excess of what many viral videos receive.

Which is why it would be interesting to see the origins of these viral videos.

On 22 May 2007, Howard Davies Carr uploaded a 56-second video featuring his two sons—Harry and Charlie—seated on a chair, where the one-year-old Charlie bit his three-year old brother's finger. Howard wanted to share the video with the boys' grandfather in the US, and he chose YouTube because the file size was too long to be sent by email.

In no time, the video went viral. In less than ten months, the video garnered more than twelve million views. In March 2010, *Time* magazine rated the video as no. 1 in their list of 'YouTube's 50 Greatest Viral Videos'.

The family also went on to have a partnership with a meme management company the next year, which served the rights to the company to use the video in meme advertisements for other brands.

Fourteen years and millions of views later, the video was auctioned in 2021 as an NFT for a sum of $7,60,399.[7] The Davies Carr family has earned hundreds of thousands of dollars from the video through sponsorships and advertising.

...

A little more than a year before the viral video of Charlie was sold as an NFT, a machine operator at a factory located in Turin, Italy, was laid off. When the Covid-19 pandemic began in early 2020, Italy was one of the first countries to be impacted.

The laid off worker did what most of the human population did, especially during the early days of the pandemic—dancing and playing video games. He also started recording TikTok videos showcasing his indoor activity.

So far, so good.

Eventually, the twenty-year old gained popularity with his 'stitch' and 'duet' videos, where he recorded video responses to complicated life-hack videos, performing tasks in a simple way—without speaking, only using hand gestures.

If you find yourself nodding your head, recalling one of the videos by none other than Khaby Lame, you have got it right.

In August 2023, Khaby was the most followed creator on TikTok worldwide. In 2022, he was listed in *Fortune* magazine's '40 under 40' and *Forbes* Magazine's '30 under 30'.

A creator rising to virality also brings virality to multiple brands they collaborate with. That's exactly the case with Khaby Lame. He collaborates with brands for endorsements and advertising, charging up to $7,50,000 per TikTok.

The list of brands he has collaborated with includes Xbox, Netflix, Amazon Prime, Dream 11, Juventus and more.

'It's my face and my expressions which make people laugh,' Khaby says about his muted reactions, stating they are a 'global language'.

...

A couple of years later, in mid of 2023, a viral Barbie emerged—a brand that has long been mired in controversies. These include the unrealistic hourglass figure, the Barbie song that oversexualized the character with remarks from Ken that objectified her, making the lyrics unsuitable for children, and the girl who didn't like mathematics, which raised eyebrows of educators who feared it would reinforce the stereotype discouraging girls from studying math and science.

However, in 2023, the brand did an excellent job of promoting the movie *Barbie*, which went on to gross $162 million in its opening weekend. From the social media chatter, which included collaborations with brands such as Airbnb, Forever 21, Burger King, or a selfie generator, or having your favorite influencer dressed up in pink to go for the *Barbie* movie, the brand led the social media strategy at the top of its marketing game, and literally left no stone unturned.

The result?

The movie grossed $1.4 billion worldwide, making it the highest-grossing movie of 2023, the highest grossing film ever released by Warner Bros, and the fourteenth highest-grossing movie of all time.

The movie received eight Academy Award nominations and won the Best Original Song award, both at Academy and the Golden Globe Awards. The movie was awarded the Golden Globe Award for Cinematic and Box Office Achievement.

Becoming viral and leveraging that to build a brand is not used on the offensive but also on defensive.

While Barbie played on the offence after perhaps playing on the defence for years, some brands have done a great job at playing on the defence.

'Meet me at the mountain's peak and bring a new coat,' a hiker by the name Jensen created a TikTok video, 'soaked' in rain, wearing a waterproof jacket from outdoor clothing brand North Face with DryVent fabric. Despite that, she still got soaked.

The video quickly went viral, earning over 11.6 million views and thousands of comments, with one person commenting, 'North Face has left the conversation.'

In no time, the team at North Face (read about skier Jossi Wells) grabbed a new jacket from a North Face store, jumped on a helicopter and delivered the new jacket to Jensen. This video again garnered over 4 million views and thousands of comments, including one from Jensen.[8]

The brand not only cared about the customer but also created huge brand loyalty through their 'quick' customer service.

. . .

There are countless things that change when your content goes viral—sometimes fun, sometimes fame, and often, money.

When we speak of virality, one of the classic examples is Nancy Tyagi. Daughter of a TV technician, Tyagi is now known for her DIY outfits, creating lookalike costumes of the top stars of the Indian movie fraternity and her famous walk at the 77th edition of Cannes Film Festival in France, in 2024.[9]

Hailing from Baranwa, a small town in the state of Uttar Pradesh in India, Nancy Tyagi moved to New Delhi to prepare for civil service exams. However, fate had a different script when Covid struck. Locked up in her home, she started creating fashion content on Instagram.

Nancy started as a self-taught designer and began creating content featuring her DIY outfits. She did not get much engagement for a year. But in 2023, things changed when she created a series called '100 outfits from scratch for 100 days'.

What started as backlash eventually propelled Tyagi to fame. In 2024, she attended the Cannes Film Festival, where she walked the red carpet in her self-designed outfit. Using 1000 metres of fabric weighing twenty kilograms, the twenty-three-year-old girl wore her own outfit and gave interviews in her mother tongue, Hindi.

Her goal?

Nancy's mother used to work in a coal factory and her only aim was to have her mother quit her hazardous job. Now, she aims to work as a fashion designer. Oh, by the way like most Indians, she also flew her ready-to-eat food from India, because, well, let's say this is how most Indians are.

When someone like Nancy rises to fame purely through passion and hard work, without the backing of an influential godfather, it becomes a fairy tale for everyone. Stories like these give wings to thousands of other aspiring girls.

The Formula for Going Viral

We all know why we are here. You are spending your valuable time on this book because you are here to understand the 'how' of everything we spoke about, including virality.

Malcolm Gladwell, who is a multiple time *New York Times* bestselling author, says, 'There is a simple way to package information that, under the right circumstances, can make it irresistible. All you have to do is find it.'

It leads to a common question: What is that formula?

I believe the formula is all that we will be discussing in great detail throughout this book:

Consistency. Focusing on a niche audience. Writing content from the point of view of the 3Rs (Relatability, Relevancy, Recency: more on this in chapter 2), and to think of another quote from Adam Braun, founder of Pencils of Promise:

To create one contagious movement, you often have to create many small movements first.

Because, let's be objective.

You go to a creator's profile via their viral content, but when you arrive on their profile, you realize—they were just following a viral trend; the original content that they create is nothing related to what you want to consume.

So, you may not end up following them.

Thus, virality is just a product of staying true to the process and reaping some more benefits than usual when virality is finally achieved.

Don't take my word for it—take it from Simon Sinek, who says, 'The best virality comes from inspiring others, not from chasing numbers.'

Marketing guru Seth Godin adds, 'Virality isn't about getting the most people to see something; it's about getting the right people to share it.'

So, my friend, if you are creating content for the right audience, virality isn't a probability; it is going to be a possibility. And I do not know of any creator who has been consistently creating content keeping their audience in mind, who hasn't gone viral at least multiple times in their journey.

The question is not 'if'. The question is 'when'. The answer is the process. The answer lies in the right science, not in pure dependence on luck. The answer is our conversations throughout the book, which we will unlock one chapter at a time.

Key takeaways:

- Virality has changed the lives of many creators. It continues to do so. From Ed Sheeran struggling to play his chords to composing one of the most viewed songs on YouTube, virality has made India the biggest market for the singer.

- Not only creators, but brands also have the opportunity to go viral, especially if they can connect with customers by joining the social chatter.
- You cannot have time or create virality. However, the more you show up consistently as a creator, the more you increase your chances of going viral.

Chapter 1(e)

Creators and Communities

Which brings us to the power of communities.

The reason social media has brought all of us together is because it gives us what our primal nature is: To find people who are exactly like us. Who think like us. Who go through the same pains and pleasures as us. Who are looking for the same solutions as us. Who wants to stand out in the world and yet fit in with people like them.

As early as 1978, more than twenty-five years before the advent of Facebook, Ward Christensen, member of the Chicago Area Computer Hobbyists' Exchange (CACHE), founded the Bulletin Board System (BBS), where users could connect, view messages from other users and post their own messages. Accessible through phone lines and designed to prevent high phone bills, BBS really took off as it connected computer users across a distributed network.

The next evolution came almost two decades later with the advent of chat rooms. Chat rooms enabled messaging (an extrapolation of direct messaging over social media platforms that we use today) between distributed users, or strangers. There were open one-to-many public chat rooms as well as private messaging features.

As an extension of chat rooms, where we could chat one-on-one, came one-to-many chat platforms—through forums and messaging boards that quickly evolved into Q&A platforms; Think Quora (where a user asks a question and experts respond, both visible to the public) and forum-like discussion platforms like Reddit (which has a decentralized moderation system).

With communities (one-to-many and one-to-one) came the advent of personalization and blogging sites. By then, celebrities had started jumping on the bandwagon and creating their own blogs. The creator ecosystem started way before the Creator Economy could take its shape.

Thus, in 2005, with YouTube and other social media platforms coming over, the reach a user could get on platforms came to be higher than blogs, turning all creators curious and serious about social media.

Amid the thread of unfolding and stitching together from the first BBS to the first video, to TikTok and viral posts everywhere, what has remained constant is human beings' affiliation with communities. 'We're all in this together' comes from the superhit movie *High School Musical*. Coincidentally, the movie was released in 2006, which was the 'start of something new' (another song from the same movie) for social media.

This affinity to togetherness in unprecedentedly hyperconnected world is what makes me optimistic about the Creator Economy.

Since the global COVID-19 pandemic hit the world in 2020, more than 165 million creators have joined the Creator Economy, with every one in four people (23 per cent) contributing to photography, videography, creative writing, and more across online spaces, including social media platforms and blogs.

To this day, I don't know anyone who does not know a creator in their closest circle. They may not be creators themselves, but they are certainly surrounded by some—both big and small creators.

This perspective makes me think of the present as fertile soil. The future resembles a dense Amazon rainforest, offering space for everyone, even though each individual is unique in their own way.

Which is what we will explore in the coming pages.

Key takeaways:

- Web 1.0 was a one-way interaction, where what we saw on a computer screen was essentially a digital brochure.
- When Web 2.0 emerged, what began as one-to-many content sharing eventually evolved, with creators and brands forming strong bonds with strangers and becoming a part of their own virtual communities.
- As the popular *High School Musical* songs go: It's the start of something new; where we're all in this together.

Chapter 2

Globalization of Content

Cricket is a religion in India. When I say this, I mean it in all my senses.

The sport unites people from left and right wings, elite or middle class, travelling by first class or by public bus, etc.

Whether it is to celebrate a World Cup victory or to lament the loss from a much-expected win that turned into a loss, watching the games is a personal and emotional experience. India has won only two World Cups in the 50-over international format and two in the T20 format.

India winning the T20 World Cup in 2024 was special in many ways.

Records were broken. New milestones were set. Teams and players rose to the forefront.

I want to speak about a team most cricket fans would have never expected to perform in the tournament:

Team USA.

For most of cricketing history, the continents of North and South America have remained distant from the sport, with the exception of Trinidad and Tobago, known as 'West Indies' in the cricketing world.

Thus, when the Canada and USA team participated in the T20 World Cup 2024, expectations weren't particularly high.

And bam! They proved everyone wrong.

Three major things that stood out for me:

1. USA hosted the tournament (along with the West Indies). It was a part of efforts to help develop and promote cricket in the United States, where the sport's fan base is primarily made up of people of south Asian origin. It was a positive move for the sport in the country, as USA hadn't hosted many international cricket matches before.

2. USA reached the Super 8 of the tournament—the qualifying round featuring the top eight teams based on their performance. The more surprising part is that Pakistan, which was in the same group as USA and has been playing cricket for the same time as the world champions India, failed to reach the Super 8.

3. One of the bowlers of the USA team, Saurabh Netravalkar, is a full-time Oracle employee. He took leave from work to be able to play in the tournament. The best part, though, is this: In the league match between USA and India, Saurabh dismissed cricketing legend Virat Kohli for a duck. Not to forget, Kohli was the top scorer in the Indian Premier League just before the World Cup and was named player of the tournament in the 2023 World Cup. Generations won't forget that a cricketer from a country playing their first ever World Cup did this. A feat perhaps Saurabh won't forget for the longest time.

While the USA team could not make it to the semi-finals, the tournament demonstrated how fluid the world is. We are all just living in the same world, distinguished merely by passports and some political opinions.

Following USA's performance, the world was quite different for world champions India back home, for three reasons:

The Indian cricket team had suffered a crushing loss in the World Cup final just seven months earlier, after an extraordinary performance throughout the tournament. The taste of victory after the shocking 'recent' loss is perhaps even sweeter.

Like we spoke before, cricket is truly a religion in India. People often find themselves in a bad state of mind when the country loses an important match. Thus, an achievement in that sport is as 'relevant' to them as their career graph with an upward trajectory.

As we speak of victory, when people see that up close in their own country, it becomes 'relatable'. After all, we've all experienced our own personal conquests of metaphorical Everests and know how it feels when victory finally comes after years of hard work.

The 3Rs (Recency, Relevancy, Relatability) that played a role in India's major 'national' victory, along with the fourth R of religion, also sparked a wave of citizen journalism. Citizen journalism, as we'll explore later in the chapter, is when people like you and I, who are not professional journalists, capture news events and share it. In this case, the 'religious followers' of cricket engaged in some citizen journalism.

The final match of the World Cup was held in Barbados, Trinidad and Tobago. Four days later, when the Indian team returned to their homeland, they had an entire day planned for them—starting with breakfast with the Prime Minister in Delhi, followed by an evening rally for the public in Mumbai, and another event in the famous Wankhede Cricket Stadium later.

It was reported that more than 3,00,000 people thronged Marine Drive to click pictures and videos of the cricketers. These included people from top firms or those with respectable positions in corporations, yet flying to Mumbai on ridiculously expensive last-minute flights, just to catch a glimpse of the victory parade. We did mention religion, didn't we?

The victory parade of the Indian Cricket Team at Marine Drive in Mumbai, five days after winning the T20 World Cup 2024 in Barbados. The road show was attended by an estimated 3,00,000 people.
Source: X/ @ompsyram

Another fan climbed up a tree just because he wanted to see Virat Kohli closely.[1]

Other fans recorded videos cheering for Hardik Pandya in Wankhede stadium, the same stadium of his home team, Mumbai Indians, where he was constantly booed in the Indian Premier League two months earlier.[2]

And just for fun, some fans chanted the name of BCCI (Board of Control of Cricket in India) President Jay Shah.[3]

The three pillars that we observed in the 2024 World Cup—of the game being fluid to not only reach the Americas but also making them exemplary performers, the 3Rs of content, and citizen journalism in action, speak volumes about globalization of content.

Let us explore in detail how.

Chapter 2(a)

Content Fluidity

I was born and raised in India. Growing up in the early 1980s, there was a show called *Chitrahaar* on our national television, Doordarshan, which aired Bollywood songs at a fixed time, from 12.30 p.m. to 6 p.m.

For my sister and me, the show was the only source of access to music. Meanwhile, in the west, the launch of MTV revolutionized the entire music industry. In fact, Michael Jackson's album *Thriller*, released in 1982—just a year after the launch of MTV—remains one of the most popular albums of all time.

Mind you, this was the 1980s. But the 1990s and early 2000s were no different.

Today, content can cross boundaries instantly and reach people, even in the most remote parts of the world.

Canadian singer Bryan Adams and American rock acts Bon Jovi and Aerosmith performed in India in the early 2000s, long before Lady Gaga, Jay-Z, Justin Bieber and Coldplay could carry the legacy of big concerts forward in the following decades.

But why is this important for us to know?

Because content migration across different parts of the globe became more seamless, giving rise to content fluidity. This is evident in how Taylor Swift and Ed Sheeran have hundreds of thousands (probably millions) of fans in Asia. Fun fact: Ed Sheeran even claims that India is his biggest market.[4]

On the other hand, we also see a lot of Asian composers succeeding in the west and having houseful concerts and even topping charts. Sure, it's nothing compared to Taylor Swift, who is boosting economies. However, the water is getting out of its original territory for sure.

A wonderful example that comes to mind is the South African singer Tyla, who gained virality with her song 'Water' in 2023, at the age of 21. She eventually went on to become the youngest African artist to win a Grammy Award. She also earned nominations for a ton of other prestigious music awards all around the globe.

It also reminds me of the Korean pop song 'Gangnam Style' by South Korean rapper Psy. Released in July 2012, the song not only debuted number one on South Korea's charts, but its music video also went viral worldwide in August 2012. In the United States, the song peaked at number two on the Billboard Hot 100, making it the highest-charting song by a South Korean artist.

By the end of 2012, 'Gangnam Style' had topped the music charts of more than thirty countries, won the Best Video at the MTV Europe Music Awards, went on to influence parodies and reaction videos by other creators, and (hold your breath) in December of the same year, it became the first YouTube video to reach a billion views!

While we are talking about Korean content, we cannot ignore the super popular Netflix show *Squid Game*. A series of nine episodes, the show featured a secret contest between 456 people. *Squid Game* went on to become Netflix's most-watched series and the most-watched programme in 94 countries, attracting more than 142 million member households and 1.65 billion viewing hours in its first four weeks, surpassing *Bridgerton* as the service's most-watched show.

A fun fact: The writer Hwang Dong-hyuk came up with the story back in 2009 but struggled to find a production company to fund the idea until Netflix took an interest around 2019, as part of a drive to expand their foreign programming offerings. Talk about right timing.

It just takes one exception to change things in entirety, doesn't it?

The 2000s, as we saw in the previous chapter, witnessed the rise of social media platforms with Facebook and YouTube dominating the scene.

The next decade saw two major revolutions:

1. The rise of OTT (Over the top) platforms such as Netflix, Amazon Prime, Hulu, which offered on-demand content, disrupting the traditional television and film industries.

2. The rise of the Creator Economy, with social media platforms enabling users to create content and generate diversified income streams through ad revenue and brand collaborations, selling products and services (for merchandise and courses to personal beauty—the list is literally endless), or by becoming affiliate partners, turning content creation into a full-time career.

A notable acceleration also happened to the Creator Economy when the Covid-19 pandemic hit the entire world in 2020.

- As the world was 'working' on their screens, it was a good time for content creators to make the best use of the increased screen time.

- People weren't going out for entertainment and could only consume it on social media.

- As many worked from home, they had more time to explore content creation as a side gig, eventually turning it into a full-time career.

- Unfortunately, this period also saw layoffs, and as a result, many people discovered their creative potential, embracing the Creator Economy as a full-time career path. Khaby Lame is a perfect example.

The entire world went through this change together. And since 2020, more than 165 million creators have joined the Creator Economy.[5] As a matter of fact, over 1 in 2 (52 per cent creators) started posting social content from 2020.[6]

Out of the total population of the US (328 million), approximately 25 per cent (86 million) are creators. In Brazil, the number is 105 million (50 per cent of its population), in Australia 6 million (23 per cent), in South Korea 52 million (34 per cent), and in India 80 million (around 5 per cent of its population).[7]

This picture of the content world is entirely different from the picture of *Chitrahaar* (*chitra* meaning picture in Hindi) I grew up with.

It's promising. It's powerful.

It's purposeful.

Most importantly, it's pervasive.

Just like water.

As the water takes the shape of the vessel it is in and the form it is being used, whether it is ice in a drink or super warm for your morning coffee, great content also finds a way to transcend all boundaries and oceans.

Whether it is 'Gangnam Style' or a Japanese anime that captivates audiences in every nook and corner of the globe, the viral Kala Chashma reel trend, or even wordless content by Khaby Lame, which made him one of the most followed creators on TikTok.

When we know that the content you have on your smartphone is the same as Elon Musk has access to in his smartphone. You have a lot more power than you think.

In the next chapter, we will explore how.

Key takeaways:

- In the pre-internet era, content accessibility was limited and dependent on the country you lived in. Or maybe your country did have access to global content, albeit quite delayed. It reminds me of the days when I joined a popular broadcast company early in my media career. During my induction, I was taken to a large studio room with multiple screens, where the dubbing of international shows used to take place. Along with dubbing, Indian ads were inserted into the 'final output of 30 minutes'. It turns out, the content wasn't freshly made. It had already been produced and telecast in the west, probably months ago, and was now being catered to domestic audiences.

- Rise of OTT, rise of social media and incremental rise in internet consumption during the pandemic led to content being fluid across geographies and continents. Unlike waiting for months like we used to back in the early 2000s, content was accessible at the click of a button.

- More than 50 per cent of content creators (165 million of 303 million[8]) started their content creation journey in 2020.

- Life used to be different when people with more resources had access to more useful information than people who lacked them. Now content is more accessible across demographics, changing a lot of things in the Creator Economy world.

Chapter 2(b)

ViRRRality and What It Means to You and I

After working with Meta in south-east Asia for several years, it was a great opportunity for me to move to the Bay Area in 2022. During my first year, I was on my way back from lunch at a friend's place at San Ramon on a warm Saturday afternoon in late July 2023. I decided to take the Bay Area Rapid Transit (BART) from Dublin/Pleasanton station to the San Francisco Bay Area. When I reached the BART station, I had the weirdest experience ever.

Every girl was dressed in glitter, a whole lot of bling. But I was in for more surprises. I could also see middle-aged women and even three generations of a family dressed the same way. Even the men were dressed like Ken from Barbie.

Which is when it occurred to me that it cannot be a hen party.

Oh wait, this was the crowd going to the Levi's Stadium in Santa Clara, which was hosting a concert of Taylor Swift's Eras Tour that evening.

Now I got it.

These people were not only swiftly moving towards a destination, but they were also Swifties (a term used to describe Taylor Swift fans). And for what might be once a lifetime event for most of these, they wanted to look their best on the day they 'met' Taylor Swift.

Maybe a unique way of saying, 'It's me, hi!'

By the way, it turns out that the mayor of Santa Clara had explicitly warned fans not to drive to the shows on 28 and 29 July. Not only that, a special train to the stadium (also called Swiftie Express) was launched for Swift's two-day stay in the San Francisco Bay Area.[9]

However, if we pause and really think about it: What is it about the Taylor Swift tour that drives everyone, across all generations, crazy?

She appeals to her audience in three ways:

1. She is relatable: Her songs don't promise a fairy tale. Most of her songs are a venting vehicle. Because at a certain level, we all need to vent out, and that is why many find her relatable. At the same time, Swift does not project an image of herself as elite, the richest, or unreachable. She brings herself down to documentation of her most vulnerable self in her songs, which brings the masses closer to her.

    While I saw families flock together for her concert, most of the audience were girls in their pre-30s years. This is also the time many people go through heartbreaks and experience their 'my boy was a montage' as well as 'you're so gorgeous' era.

    As one of the readers wrote, 'Sometimes, her lyrics hit so close to home that you feel like she knows exactly what is going on in your relationship.'[10]

    But this is not entirely it. She is also the friend next door who literally invites you to her home. It is suggested that Swift ranks very high on the list of stars who treat their fans the best.

2. She is relevant: Whether she likes it or not, Taylor Swift has become 'a pillar of the cultural zeitgeist',

embodying love, diligence and feminism, says a popular magazine. Other top platforms have described Swift as an 'American treasure', 'the most famous and influential cultural icon', and 'synonymous with American pop culture'. The *Washington Post* has also gone on to say that Swift and the Super Bowl are two of the most beloved phenomena in American culture. One cultural critic said that Swift 'wears the American flag on her face'—red lips, white skin and blue eyes.

However, as someone with an audience-only-but-creator-economy-experience-driven view of Swift, I also think relevance is a result of staying in the game long enough. Longer than anyone has the right to think that you have the right to stay in the game.

Swift, no doubt, has excelled like nobody else.

Time magazine included Swift on its 2010, 2015 and 2019 rankings of the '100 most influential people'. In 2014, she was named in *Forbes*' '30 Under 30' list in the music category. Swift became the youngest woman to be included on *Forbes*' list of the '100 most powerful women in 2015', ranked at number sixty-four, and the first entertainer to ever be placed in the list's top five in 2023. She was the most Googled woman in 2019 and musician in 2022, as well as the most Googled songwriter of all time. Media outlets have noted that she reached a new zenith of fame in 2023, with *Glamour* saying she 'has officially taken over every aspect of popular culture'. Describing a critical consensus, another journalist said Swift is 'increasingly being spoken about as an economic force of nature, a transformative creator advocate, organizer and innovator and arguably the most influential and even the most powerful figure in the music industry'.

I could go on and on and rave about how Swift has stayed relevant for close to two decades, and still goes on to redefine success every single place she steps in. Well, I guess Swift was right when she metaphorically called herself 'Miss Americana' in her 2019 song 'Miss Americana & the Heartbreak Prince', which also inspired the namesake 2020 documentary about her life and career.[11]

3. The most recent tour of hers: The Eras Tour was her first tour in five years. *New Yorker* goes on to say that the concept of the concert is autobiographical: Swift looks back at her career, album by album, each of which she ascribes to a different 'era' in her life and each of which constitutes a segment of the show.[12]

    Let us also be pragmatic and think about it:

    When will Taylor Swift next tour the world for all of her albums again?

    We don't know. No one does. So, all we have is now.

    On a very unrelated note, let me quote the great author Eckhart Tolle, who says in his legendary book *The Power of Now*: 'Realise deeply that the present moment is all you have. Make the NOW the primary focus of your life.'

    Well, Taylor Swift fans won't disagree.

    …

It turns out, since millions have been a part of the Eras tour, whether through attending the concert or attending the prelude like me or coming across fan videos on Instagram where thousands say 'hi' in unison followed by 'It's me', I also believe this 3R concept has a lesson for the Creator Economy.

However, why is this 3R concept (Relatable-Relevant-Recent) important for you and I?

Before I go on to explain the lesson for the Creator Economy, it would be prudent to listen to someone who has been in the Creator Economy for more years than anyone else.

Seth Godin, who happens to be one of the world's leading marketers, author of more than twenty *New York Times* bestsellers, pioneer of ethical online direct marketing[13] and a daily blogger for over twenty-five years, has a signature statement that says:

People like us do things like this.[14]

Godin goes on to say, 'There is no more powerful tribal marketing connection than this'.

More than features, more than benefits, we are driven to become a member in good standing of the tribe. We want to be respected by those we aspire to connect with, we want to know what we ought to do to be part of that circle.

Not the norms of mass, but the norms of our chosen tribe.

A good piece of content that is relatable, relevant and recent does exactly that. It brings like-minded people together and acts as a unifier.

If we take a broader view, now virtually everything around us is content.

A walk in the park that gives you droolworthy pictures for Instagram. Discussing with your team about how to become more productive with the same resources could go on to become a LinkedIn post. An offline store owner selling ice cream and using his persuasion skills to drive more sales.

At the same time, those are only events in isolation.

What brings us together is the amalgamation of all these three pillars, acting as a unifier for those consuming it.

Let's understand it in detail:

Relevant Content

It addresses the core need of the audience at that *time*, and hence, keeps them invested. This is where they are most likely to act.

We call it the 'hand' connection with the audience. Relevant content gets the audience to move their hand, i.e., act. For example, if you are looking to buy a new car and you start getting ads on your social media for exactly that car, the content is relevant to you. It won't be relevant to your neighbour who bought a new car just six months back. But for you, it is a topic of a thesis.

Relatable Content

This kind of content connects with the audience at a deeper level, directly addressing their emotions. It is where their hearts truly lie. A relatable content piece appeals to a hidden or active emotion within us and connects to us in ways perhaps the content creator would not have thought.

The 1997 film *Titanic* addressed the emotion of love beyond all barriers, and hence, was relatable.

Memes that go viral address the human emotions of just wanting to have fun. Dog videos that are loved by people who are not dog parents address the common need of companionship, faithfulness and fun; thus, connecting at a core level.

Recent Content

It tackles the issues that are top-of-mind for the audience. A content piece that is up-to-date or the latest one in the series of events.

This is where the audience's mind is stuck, and we refer to it as the connection with 'head'.

Tim Cook talking about Apple Vision Pro at the latest Apple event is a 'recent piece of content', whether the last event took place yesterday or eleven months ago. On the other hand, Steve Jobs launching the first iPhone is relatable to most, relevant to a few and recent to none.

A point to be noted is that recency does not mean as recent as yesterday. It simply means what is recent in the context of the content we are speaking about.

On a platform like X, 'recent' means as little as a few hours. On Instagram, it might mean a few days at maximum. On YouTube, depending on the consistency of the channel, 'recent' may mean a week or a few weeks or perhaps a few months. On a blog sharing review on tech products, 'recent' may mean up to a few months or perhaps a year or two old, till the next in latest development catches up.

Recency is contextual, and hence, affects what is relatable and relevant as well.

...

As we connect the 3Hs of the human body with the three Rs of the content industry, we get 3HRs (no human resources, just the resources for content):

Hand: Relevant

Heart: Relatable

Head: Recent

For a human body to function fully well, all three elements—head, heart and hands (or limbs)—need to be coordinated, in sync, and working at full capacity.

Similarly, for a content body or a content piece to function effectively, it needs to be at the intersection of recency, relatability and relevance.

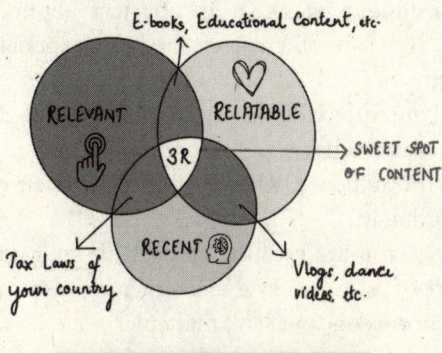

THE 3-R CONTENT FRAMEWORK

While we understand the three pillars of content that unify it, how do they come together to create that experience?

If you are someone looking to cook delicious desserts at home during any festive season, a food vlogger's video titled 'Make healthy tasty desserts at home during festivals in less than 20 minutes' does the trick.

It is relevant to you because you want to prepare desserts. It gets you in 'doing mode'.

It is relatable because you want to do it in the minimum time possible. It appeals to your emotions (heart).

It is recent because you want to prepare desserts during the festive time, which is when the content piece was produced by the creator.

A content piece that ticks all these boxes acts as a unifier, and hence, helps in building communities.

What does it mean to you and I who have been scrolling reels for over three hours when we intended to spend only ten minutes, or to you as a creator considering content creation as a career?

It turns out that creating content from the 3Rs content framework leads to creating a unifying experience, which eventually helps in building communities.

It is this power of shared connections online that make people consume content. It is not just about the content any more. It is about creators creating experiences around that content.

Thus, content creation is no longer a stand-alone process where you share what you want to share, rather you build it along with the audience, where you listen to their response and create accordingly.

In a way, you are creating along with your audience. In a strange sort of way, you as a consumer are also the co-creator of the Creator Economy. Isn't that epic?

Not until you want to think of classic cult examples like Harry Potter or Barbie.

Do they also fit into the relevant-recent-relatable criteria? But Harry Potter didn't come out yesterday. It has been there for more than two decades. And Barbie has been around since the 1950s.

Here is how I would explain it:

Barbie is a continuous cultural phenomenon. It is going to be recent always, because she is a part of the growth of how cultural sentiments can keep on going and grow along with us. Even if we outgrow Barbie physically. That's for Harry Potter too. It is not recent any more. But it has ingrained itself so much that it is a part of our pop culture. Oh, by the way, for anyone picking up a Harry Potter book or a Barbie doll because they are in that 'age/customer' criteria, it is recent for them too!

They also relate to us personally. Not the person we show in corporate life, but the people who we are for real. They reflect our dreams, struggles, and sense of identity in ways that go beyond fiction. Relatability strikes deep. It isn't just about trends; it's about how deeply something resonates with our personal journey.

At the same time, relevance isn't just about being widely known; it's about why something matters. Both Barbie and Harry Potter give people courage, hope, and a way to express themselves. They help us stand for who we are, not in a surface-level way, but in a way that connects to our deeper selves.

Which is why, if a piece of content has percolated the barriers of years and fears to be there for you in your yearning as well as frowning, it's because it has always passed the criteria of 3Rs.

Be it Taylor Swift's latest tour, or a movie that was released decades ago, and everything in between, before and after that.

To summarize all of that, a content creator who creates relevant, relatable and recent content goes on to create engaged communities. Such engaged communities transform random first-time consumers into loyal participants, and eventually, into buyers and evangelists.

Here is how:

1. The content creator creates content keeping in mind the relevant, relatable and recent aspects of it.

2. Understanding audience behaviour through data—identifying what resonates with them the most.

3. Doing more of what the audience resonates with.

4. Rinse and repeat, thus, leading to building a strong community of fans. They are not just audiences; they know the creator and resonate with them.

5. That fan turns into a super fan.

6. The super fan turns into a customer, bringing in more customers. This superfan also goes on to be more engaged on other platforms of the same creator, such as newsletters, podcasts, maybe upcoming merchandise and events.

7. The flywheel continues, thus bringing in inputs from all parts of the machine—the creator creates more content across formats that resonate with the audience, the audience giving them feedback, becoming customers, bringing in more, and on and on.

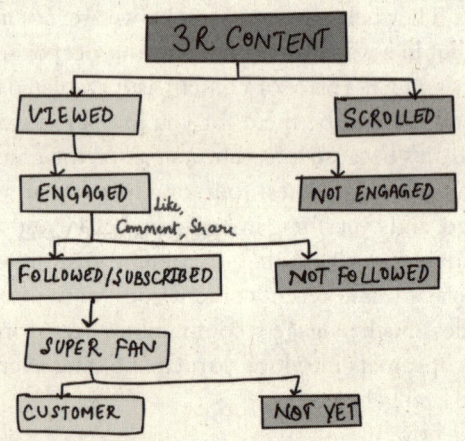

It is like people walking into a mall. Not every walk-in human is a customer, but through similar cycles of penetration, some are.

Here's an example:

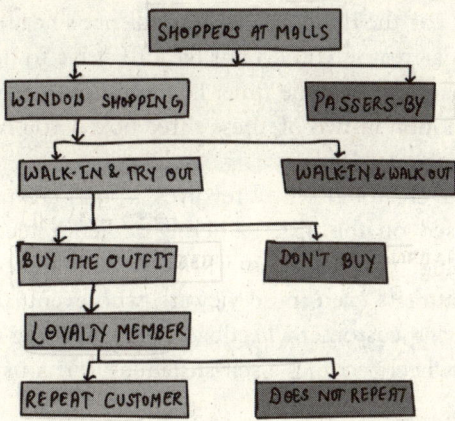

Content that is relatable and relevant automatically builds communities that fuses through all cultures and barriers.

A community of driven consumers not only pushes the content creator forward, but it also pushes the Creator Economy forward, as we will explore in the next chapter.

As good and hopeful as joining forces of content are, the repercussions of content being a unifier for big news moments aren't small either. We will walk through it in the next chapter in detail.

Key takeaways:

- The best content that blows up the internet often consists of three useful elements:
  - Relatable: It connects to the audience at a deeper level. (Their hearts)
  - Relevant: It is something useful to them. (It is something they can act on. It is in their hands.)
  - Recent: As the word suggests, something that happened in a close moment in history would have

more relevance than the same event happening eons back. (It is something new, so to say at the top of the mind, i.e., in the audience's head)

- As a creator, you do not have to strive to tick all three boxes at the same time. However, even if you invoke emotion in two of these three boxes, you have mostly hit the nail.

- The creator flywheel revolves around creating content based on the 3Rs, gathering audience feedback, and doing more of what works. As the audience grows, it attracts even more viewers, who eventually become paying customers. Feedback keeps flowing in, and the flywheel becomes a self-sustaining, virtuous cycle.

Chapter 2(c)

Big News Moments

'The bottom line is, it was long enough to kill him, (it was) long enough to execute him.'[15]

A little before 8 p.m. on 25 May 2020, a drunk man went to purchase cigarettes at Cup Foods, a grocery store at the intersection of East 38th Street and Chicago Avenue, in Minneapolis's Powderhorn Park neighbourhood in Minnesota state of the United States.

He paid with a $20 bill, which an employee realized was counterfeit after the man's exit from the store. The employees approached the man while he was in his vehicle and demanded he return the cigarettes, which he refused.

A store employee, in turn, called the police to report the fake bills. The store owner wanted to make sure there was no crime being committed.

This is where the story of the brutal homicide of George Floyd began, which, in turn, led to the social movement of 'Black Lives Matter' in the United States, with 15–26 million people participating in the movement, making it one of the largest movements in the country's history.

What happened at Cup Foods that day that led to such a massive movement?

It turned out, four police officers arrived by 8.17 p.m. at the location, and by 8.19 p.m., one of the police officers, Chauvin, pulled Floyd outside of the vehicle when he fell to the pavement.

It was seen that Chauvin was kneeling on Floyd's neck, while another officer applied pressure to his torso. The third officer was pressing down on Floyd's legs, and a fourth officer stood nearby.

The encounter of 8 minutes and 45 seconds was recorded by Darnella Frazier, a seventeen-year-old present at the scene.[16]

At 8:29 p.m., Floyd was wheeled into the ambulance and was declared dead at 9:25 p.m. at the Hennepin County Medical Center emergency room in Minnesota.

As a result of this, mass protests took place in as many as 2,000 cities all over the world, demanding justice for George Floyd and as a demonstration against the police brutalities that people of colour faced.

A year later, in June 2021, the teen who recorded the footage went on to receive the Pulitzer Prize, which is regarded as the highest national honour in print journalism, literary achievement, and musical composition in the United States.[17] The special citation was awarded to her for courageously recording the murder of George Floyd, a video that spurred protests against police brutality around the world, highlighting the crucial role of citizens in journalists' quest for truth and justice.

Here's the most fascinating part, though:

Darnella was a high school junior at the time of Floyd's murder, who just happened to be present at the scene, She was not a professional journalist.

This is an example of citizen journalism and how it highlighted the importance of eyewitness accounts on police violence, using technology to hold authorities accountable for their actions.

Before we dig deep into how George Floyd's murder impacted journalism in the United States, let's gather a bit of understanding of what citizen journalism is.

Howstuffworks.com defines citizen journalism as 'any type of news gathering and reporting—writing and publishing articles about a newsworthy topic or posting photographs or video of a newsworthy event—that is done by members of the general public rather than the professional news agencies.'[18]

Citizen journalism, as the name suggests, is the practice of ordinary citizens recording and sharing news events they capture on their devices, sharing videos or blogs from their point of view. It is exactly where democratization of media becomes real.

With devices in the hands of every single one of us, people now have the power to contribute to the real-time coverage of news events, often capturing moments that might have otherwise gone unnoticed or were not recorded by professional broadcast journalists.

Broadcast journalism, on the other hand, refers to both traditional and modern journalism, presented by qualified journalists. The reporting of news is professionally produced through broadcasts, articles and multimedia content.

Here is how both veins of journalism differ from each other:

Key Areas	Citizen Journalism	Broadcast Journalism
Who	Individuals, not professional journalists.	Professionally trained journalists.
What	Reporting news recorded on own devices or sharing in-person blogs of the events.	Reporting news through professionally produced broadcasts, articles, and multimedia content.
How	In-person experiences, eyewitnesses, and (perhaps) unstructured reporting.	In-depth analysis, investigative reporting, and fact-checking.
Scope	Local, personal and sometimes niche events.	Covers everything - from local to international to even events of the space!
Control	Because it is done by individuals, it lacks editorial oversight.	Content is professionally crafted and goes through editoral oversight.
Example	Teen recording homicide of George Floyd, leading to movement of Black Lives Matter.	News channels covering the footage of protests of Black Lives Matter, and how it impacted the local cities and the world at large.

What impact did citizen journalism have on the reporting of George Floyd's death?[19]

1. Many journalists and news organizations were already reporting actively on race-related issues, but the incident sparked important conversations about why systemic racism really matters.

2. It was also a wake-up call for news channels who were not talking about racism in the first place.

3. It also highlighted the responsibility journalists have to accurately report on racial issues and provide context for readers.

4. Most of all, it came with a huge challenge for journalists to dig deep into historical and social factors that have been compounded, contributing to racism over the years.

5. If news organizations did understand the importance of providing accurate information, they also realized the need to prioritize diversity and inclusion, so that they brought diverse perspectives to important social issues of inequality, injustice, and also gender and identity.

As we speak about citizen journalism and how it has given more power to citizens and power to journalists, I cannot depart from this chapter without telling you the story of the 9/11 attacks of New York, that, along with being the biggest attack in the American history, also catapulted a dramatic change in the way humans report history.

At 8:46 a.m. on the morning of 11 September 2001, a rookie French filmmaker named Jules Naudet was practicing his camera work while working on a film about firefighters.

Immediately afterward, he heard the overpowering noise of an airplane, which was surprising because 'in Manhattan, you don't hear planes too often', says the video. As he raised the camera on a fluke, his lens became the only one to record the American Airlines Flight 11 hitting the North Tower of the World Trade Center, according to Kenneth T. Jackson, the president of New-York Historical Society. When the second plane hit the South Tower just a few minutes later, nearly a hundred cameras captured the attack.

With hundreds of thousands recording the aftermath of the collapse, it also went on to become the most documented event in human history.

...

Citizen journalism, however, does not, by definition, mean to capture gloom and doom events around us. It can take various shapes and forms. It could also be positive and connect us to humanity. For example, citizen journalism not only showed the hurt and loss of 9/11, but also highlighted the bravery of the people on the ground.

At the time when the towers were collapsing to the ground, people were running as far as they could to save themselves. Some videos captured shop owners asking people to get inside so they could escape being crushed under the debris of the collapsing buildings. Another video captured how a bunch of firefighters were saying a sort of 'goodbye' to each other while going up inside the buildings to rescue people. They knew they were not coming back. Though not a part of citizen journalism, in a family of nine sons, two of the firefighters' sons went on to become firefighters after witnessing their father serve during the 9/11 tragedy. 'You will never become rich, but you will be very, very happy' were the words of their father, the unsung hero, one of the hundreds of firefighters who were on duty in that unfortunate incident.

When we think about news in today's context, it is served to us on a platter of notifications, along with updates on who tagged whom in Instagram feeds. There is virtually no difference.

However, when major news moments occur, they bring responsible citizens to the forefront and make them realize the importance of the power they possess.

I shared two. There are perhaps 200 more such instances, if not 2000, of how citizens have gone on to capture news events that a broadcast journalist would be lucky to have on their radar.

But citizen journalism, that broadly comes down to power of content, also shows how movements come alive and how changes happen when citizens come together. Even when they are not supposed to. So that the world comes together and does things they are supposed to.

Key takeaways:

- Content is not always beautiful; it's not a bed of roses or just fun live streams. Sometimes, it also reveals the harsh side.
- Citizen journalism is when people like you and I, whose day job is not journalism, capture an important event with our devices and put it out on the internet.
- It does not mean we are always on the job the moment we step out of our houses. However, what it does mean is that if a situation calls for it, acting responsibly would be wise and prudent. It reminds me of one of the trips I took with my son. We were driving through the mountainous terrain in Leh (the place is 3500 metres above sea level) where I witnessed a landslide moments after we passed through it. It was a near-death experience. Yet here I am, writing this book. Well, the point is, when you are in the middle of something that might become news. you are mostly unprepared to capture it. Heck, I was carrying a professional camera along with my phone as well. However, you just go with the flow. Of protecting yourself. Citizen journalism requires more presence of mind, grit and maybe it requires more responsibility than ever.

Chapter 3

Democratization of Content

Bandra is a posh suburb in one of the most expensive cities in India, Mumbai. Well, if Shah Rukh Khan lives in the area, it has to be, right?

During my days of working with Meta in their Mumbai office, I was living in the same area, albeit in a tiny apartment.

At that time, I used to believe the Creator Economy operated from a place of privilege like Bandra, where creators had all the necessary tools and resources to tell their stories—cameras, high-speed wireless internet, a crew, etc. I nearly believed this was how the Creator Economy functioned and operated. But life has a way of surprising you one day at a time, and you end up remembering that day forever.

In 2017, I visited a part of Mumbai I never expected to travel to, as part of my job leading Media Partnerships at Meta.

The US Product Team was visiting our India office on an 'India immersion study'. They wanted to learn more about the Indian market, explore emerging trends, gain audience insights, and get a sense of the undercurrent cultures that were beginning to form in India. Basically, they had come over to understand more about India.

So, I planned to take them to some of the more established and semi-established creators and have them have one-on-one conversations with them. We also visited film studios and production houses just to give them a perspective on what the market would look like from a media standpoint.

It was during this time that someone suggested we should also take them to Dharavi to meet the members of The Dharavi Dream Project (TDDP) and provide them with a well-rounded perspective.

Dharavi, which happens to be the largest slum in India and the third largest in the world, was certainly not in my remotest agenda. However, till date, I am glad we visited that place.

So, in partnership with the Universal Media Group, India, which is a massive music label, we planned a visit to the Dharavi slum area.

Usually, you would rent a car. Not in this case, my friend.

Cars can only take you where the roads are. Reminds me of the classic quote from Dr. Emmett Brown in the *Back to the Future* trilogy: 'Roads? Where we're going, we don't need roads.'

What we were about to witness stood as a classic example of that.

In Dharavi, there were criss-crossing bylanes that could be navigated only on foot. We were a group of more than ten people, and it would be safe to say that our walking line got stretched, disrupted and dismantled several times because some of us would stop to click pictures with the locals, and others got lost in the maze of lanes.

Some 5,000 steps later, we reached a modest-looking schoolhouse. After being welcomed by the facilitator of TDDP, we met a group of fifty kids, all in the range of 5–15. I assumed they had limited financial means before getting a quick tour of the school building that did not have much other than shoulder-to-shoulder classrooms with an assembly ground that doubled as a playground.

We finally settled in one of the classrooms at the student desks, as the group went to the front and started performing.

With no electricity, our eyes acclimatized to the low natural lighting of the damp classrooms; I frankly was not expecting much. Though we were told they were a group of fabulous beatboxers and hip-hoppers, I really wasn't sure how good they were.

However, what I felt that day was something that shook me up—and it did the same to all my colleagues.

As these kids started beatboxing, they were absolutely phenomenal. I can assure you my jaw dropped.

With barely any resources, a mic gifted by someone and a tiny loudspeaker, they came up with a beatboxing set that was unmatched and unparalleled.

But this was not all. The adjoining classroom had another set of kids—hip-hoppers—equally brilliant at their craft. It was brilliant because they were bringing underground pop culture to the mainstream.

I was also exhilarated by the fact that they did not undergo formal training. Most of them were self-taught. The ones that excelled at their craft taught other kids. (Imagine the hefty dollars of consultation they didn't charge for.)

However, here is something that I absolutely loved:

Some of these kids also have their own Instagram and YouTube pages. They are content creators with active following. They even perform in concerts. Over time, they have, of course, become bigger, better funded and increased the number of their students. They now train in five different fields and have been featured on the reality show *India's Got Talent*, and also been mentored by stalwarts of the Indian music industry.

*In the image: My (then) colleagues and I at Meta after the
performance by the members of The Dharavi Dream Project*

The story is as fresh in my eyes as though it happened yesterday.
It was truly eye-opening to see their journey—from humble
beginnings to becoming musicians and creators in their own
right. An absolutely fascinating tale.

...

I share this story because it is one of the brightest examples of
how you can come from any part of the world and leave a mark
for yourself in the Creator Economy.

The Creator Economy is for everyone, from anywhere, and
built by all of us.

Which is what makes it hopeful for all of us.

In the various parts of the next chapter, we will understand
all the moving pieces of being a content creator and how many
possibilities it can open up for you.

Chapter 3(a)

The Accidental Creator

If we wrap our heads around it, being a creator could be so much fun.

Unboxing videos.

Stories of concerts of your favourite band.

GRWM (Get-Ready-With-Me) videos. Thank you, Selena Gomez.

Baby Shark being the most viewed video on YouTube across the entire platform.

If this is still not surprising enough, the only Instagram post by @world_record_egg garnered over sixty million likes and held the title of the most liked post on the platform since its upload on 4 January 2019—until 18 December 2022, when photos of Lionel Messi and the Argentina national football team celebrating their 2022 FIFA World Cup triumph surpassed it. However, the egg photo still holds the record for the longest reign as the most-liked picture on Instagram as of early 2025, maintaining the title for over 1,436 days.

Or take the twelve-year-old YouTuber Ryan Kaji, who started making videos at the age of four. As of January 2025, he has amassed more than 38 million subscribers and over 59 billion views on his channel. The channel was born from Ryan's question to his mom: why wasn't he on YouTube when other kids were. And here he is, almost a decade later, making a mark in the Creator Economy like no one else.

It is insane how much joy comes with being a creator. However, that is just one side of the coin.

Let's be honest, most creators do not reach that level of fame, popularity or virality.

Do they even have a place in this massive Creator Economy universe?

What if I told you that you can start from absolutely zero, have no connections with any creator, not be born with a silver spoon in your mouth, and still make it big as a creator?

No, I'm not joking. If I could joke, I'd have a thriving career as a stand-up comedian or perhaps a politician, I'd not be writing a book about the Creator Economy.

It is not only true, but also a fact for every big, small creator that goes big.

Because let's talk about practicality—one may be born with enough generational wealth to take care of their family for generations. What truly gets you 'big' as a creator is your skill, your craft, consistency, and a relentless drive for improvement. The best part is, you can do it even if you weren't born with a silver spoon—or maybe not even a steel one.

Which is why if you are someone who does not have any background of being affiliated with any creator, but you have the 'it' factor in you, the itch to become a creator, the art to share with all of us, no matter what medium, the Creator Economy is for you.

It is like the sea, it does not care who you are or where you come from. If you learn to dive, snorkel or swim or maybe even float, the journey is going to be a beautiful one. And perhaps a big one as well.

Which brings me to top creators. The story with your favourite big creator—whether it is MrBeast from the US or Raffi and Nagita from Indonesia, Tyla from South Africa or Tanmay Bhat in India—you probably know their stories really well.

However, I want to take you on a journey to the stories hidden in the deepest corners of the content ecosystem, still unexplored by most of us.

I am in no way stating that the creators above had an unfair advantage. No one ever has an unfair advantage in the Creator Economy because it is so new, blooming and evolving at a pace that feels like an unfair advantage in itself.

What I am trying to say is that we all know or have access to the backstories of the topmost creators of the pyramid. They are hugely inspiring and glorious in their own ways; however, I am also a huge proponent of bringing out lesser known yet incredibly inspiring stories.

Because these are the stories that make us believe that someone with lesser resources and opportunities can make it. Through the sheer power of persistence, belief in themselves and hope for the future, there is only hope and hallelujah for the rest of us.

Which brings me to the story of Gangavva Milkuri.

When we think of a woman above the age of sixty in a remote village in India, we often picture someone who had to sacrifice her own dreams and aspirations to care for her family

Born in 1962, Gangavva Milkuri was no exception.[1] With no formal education, she did farm work and rolled cigarettes to support her family. Her husband was an alcoholic; thus, she had to work harder to provide for her two daughters and a son.

However, when life handed her a chance, Gangavva restarted her journey—and she did so with a bang.

Grandmother of eight, hailing from a small village in Telangana, she is the star and the lead of *My Village Show*, a YouTube channel with 3.1 million subscribers as of early-2025.

It turns out, the channel was initially started by her son-in-law Srikanth Sriram in 2012, who happens to be a filmmaker. He would shoot plants and trees in the village, and Gangavva would think to herself, 'Why is this boy wasting his time making videos?'

Over time, she started making guest appearances in the videos, and in 2017, she became more involved in the show—marking the point when it truly took off.

Sriram confirms Gangavva is indeed very natural before the camera. Because she never had a formal education and had to quit school in the first grade, she cannot read scripts and the crew has to explain the sequence to her. However, it is this raw nature that shines brightly through her impromptu appearances.

Gangavva also boasts of an Instagram account (@gangavva) with over 3.26 lakh followers (as of early 2025) and counting. She also became a contestant of the fourth season of the reality TV show *Big Boss*, in its Telugu edition.

Talk about going from the Creator Economy to 'Create your own economy'.

Taking selfies with fans who visit the village just to meet her, Gangavva confesses, 'I like being in front of the camera, I like acting. It's nice to know that people from all over India are watching what I do.'

While the journey of Gangavva is one of applause and appreciation, I want to take a step back to break down and see what actually connected with the audience and led to this breakthrough growth.

*Gangavva in her home base—driving a tractor in
her village. Source: Gangavva on Instagram*

Here is what stood out:

- Gangavva's style of emoting comedy. I believe a lot of people of her age and generation are good at it; they just never had a platform to showcase that, or even felt that this was a skill that could be loved by audiences.
- She did not try to be someone else. She was conversing in her usual raw way. Authenticity is a superpower. Especially in a crowded Creator Economy where everyone is trying to mimic others by merely copying their success formula, instead of creating their own.
- Gangavva was not anxious about 'making it big'. She was doing it just because it was fun. Such a stellar lesson for being a creator. And for life.
- Simplicity is a superpower. When you go to the YouTube channel description of *My Village Show*, it reads:

Do you want ultimate village fun. This is a completely different youtube channel. Hi, i am sriram srikanth. Welcome to "MY VILLAGE SHOW". This channel is about my crazy thoughts in daily life surrounds by me and my village "lambadipally" near karimnagar. i love my village so much.

No fancy English, no fake promises, as a matter of fact, there is some scope to make this description a little better and of course, grammatically correct. But what clearly oozes out is simplicity, which wins the game.

More than anything else, it reminds me of a statistic by an extensive research by Adobe, which states that 48 per cent of creators are motivated by the same goal of freedom of expression.[2] Gangavva, expresses that freedom out loud and in a fun way, through every content piece she puts out.

...

As we are talking of self-expression, I can't resist sharing the story of Reesa Teesa, whose story took the internet by storm.

Reesa Teesa, a common creator who skyrocketed from 3000 followers to more than 3.6 million on TikTok in just three weeks, is the pseudonym of a thirty-nine-year-old corporate worker Tareasa Johnson. A divorcee, she shared her story of struggles, poor decisions in her love life and her journey of self-reflection in a fifty-part series on TikTok.[3]

The series is called *Who TF Did I Marry?*, where Reesa reveals how her ex turned out to be a 'pathological liar' who invented family members, staged phone conversations, and forged documents to buy a house. She adds, 'The only thing that turned out to be true was his name and date of birth.'

Since commenters resonated with her initial video and thought it was a lifetime movie, Reesa went and created a fifty-part series.

Completely raw and in diarist storytelling mode, sometimes from her car seat, and other times with curlers in her hair.

Reesa did confess that she was putting herself out there in a very vulnerable way, but I believe it was her vulnerability that made the audience connect with her.

People are often hesitant about sharing their darkest and deepest wounds with friends, family and even therapists. With the thought of not being labelled as a perpetual complainer, but her vulnerability (and maybe being aware of the repercussions sharing the truth might bring) certainly brought an emotion of, 'I believe everything you say' to many of her audiences.

Though it would not have been an easy journey for her to share, let alone go through it, she had at least twenty interviews set up on the day she appeared on *The Morning Show*, and her lawyer thought she might make $2 million in 2024 and twice the amount in 2025.

Oh yes, as of writing this, Reesa hasn't quit her job yet!

Here are a few key takeaways from Reesa's journey that could be helpful for all of us:

1. The common human emotion that binds us all is pain. When we see someone else share their pain (especially from a place of authenticity) all we see is, 'Hey, even I have been through a part of this. This seems relatable'.
2. When we are in a state of pain, we want to share the tiniest details. The audience also comes from a place of empathy and is accepting of such details. This natural human instinct to just be there from a place of concern created a relationship between Reesa and her audience.
3. We become adept at what we do repeatedly. Since most of us are consuming content on our devices for so long, we have developed an innate feel for identifying 'people who speak from the heart'. The intricacy of detail with which Reesa spoke struck a chord with her audience, leading them to believe she spoke from the heart.
4. Human beings connect on a deeper level when they realize they are not alone in what they are going through. Reesa was not only speaking her life story, but she was also unconsciously speaking parts of stories of many of her viewers.
5. Not everyone has the courage to speak up about their difficulties, especially about a relationship that has become sour. The world often rewards the brave and the courageous. Which is what Reesa Teesa got rewarded with.

Oh, by the way, actor and producer Natasha Rothwell is developing the whole thing into a TV adaptation under her production company, Big Hattie Productions. Jaw dropping moments sometimes become commonplace in the creator economy.

This conversation about starting from nowhere and then reaching heights isn't reserved for people with limited means. Since becoming a creator has many nuances (as you would see later in the book), I would want to chime in with the example of Shalini Passi here.

Passi is a Delhi-based art collector, philanthropist, and artist, founder of MASH and the Shalini Passi Art Foundation to promote art, design, and emerging talents. A UNICEF Champion for Children, she donates extensively, including proceeds from her Netflix debut Fabulous Lives vs Bollywood Wives. She's won numerous awards for her contributions.

But do you know what's the best part? Despite such massive success, Shalini does not consider herself an influencer. Even for the small collaborations she does from time to time, all the proceeds are donated to UNICEF India for their childcare missions in Purnea, Bihar.

But does Shalini Passi go through the constant pressure of being a creator? Passi is very clear that for her there is no constant pressure to put out things, because she does many different things. Even while travelling, she shares her pictures, travel pictures, pictures from museum visits, health tips or products she likes because she thinks these things will benefit people. 'Everything you see on my feed belongs to me,' says Shalini. The pressure is non-existent, because she does things not for commercial reasons, but purely out of joy.

If this didn't inspire you, I don't know what will.

For me, here are the main things I drew from Passi's journey:

1. You have a life outside of the screen first. Thus, when you go on to become a creator, if you are as authentic as Shalini, you go on to influence millions.

2. Do things to help people, instead of living under constant pressure to put yourself out there.

3. Our lives are beyond just our lives. Shalini is a giver in all respects, and her approach may inspire many well-off creators to perhaps also consider philanthropy where one part of their proceeds as a creator may nourish.

4. We are always getting started. If Shalini is getting started even at this peak, I think the lesson out there is to always remain a beginner.

5. Despite humongous success, Passi doesn't let it get to her head. The equation of karma in her mind is clear, at the same time she is a giver, giver, giver; without once talking about the idea of receiving, perhaps because all she is focused on is being a giver. I think this is how perhaps all givers operate. For others.

Key takeaways

- What makes you a 'big' creator is not generational wealth or contact with celebrities. What makes you big as a creator is having skill, an art, consistency and relentless improvement.

- If you have the 'it' factor, no matter where you come from or what you do, the Creator Economy is for you. Fun fact: Each one of us has an 'it' factor about us.

- Not only big creators (the ones with millions of followers that you secretly admire and aspire to become one day as well), but there are also creators in smaller capacities and weird talents that have created their own audience.

- Whether you are in a remote village or have never faced a camera before or debut with a Netflix special and then go on to become a creator, there is something for everyone in the Creator Economy.

- The human emotions of fun, pain, giving, purpose and everything in between drive us to connect with others.

- In the process, when we share our stories, we unconsciously share the stories of so many of our viewers.

- Being consistent and real leads to predictability of expectations and, therefore, lets the audience connect better with you.

Chapter 3(b)

The A-B-C of Everything

When we think of the Creator Economy, we already think of it as that big, vast unknown.

'I have no idea what it takes to be there' is a phrase that people repeat to themselves, in some form or another.

I'm an avid sportsperson, I am always up for a game of squash. Oftentimes, I coach younger and even aspiring adults to pick up the basics of this sport.

Often, I figure there are broadly three kinds of folks who enter the courts:

1. The ones who are intrigued by the sport and are ready to dive in, go through the rigour and put in some hours and effort in trying to learn the ropes. I call them the Actioners.
2. Then there are the Born Naturals. They have a flair for racquet sports; they just have the right posture, the correct footing and the perfect power. But even they don't sustain for long if they aren't committed to learning the basic discipline of the sport and build on their natural game through practice.
3. Lastly, there is the third category, the Curious Passers-by. They are more likely to enter the court maybe once

or twice and realize the muscle aches and pains are not worth their time and effort. Needless to say, I usually never see them on the court again.

It all really boils down to your commitment to the cause.

While Gangavva is in the category of Actioners, putting in that grunt work and building her presence through sheer grit and determination, Reesa Teesa might be in the category of Born Naturals.

What will be interesting to observe is whether she can build a lasting legacy from where she stands, through sustained and ongoing efforts. Will she embody the disciplined strides of the Creator Economy?

I share the stories of Gangavva and Reesa Teesa to state that there is scope and hope for everyone in the Creator Economy, in every part of the world. Especially if you are willing to put in hard work, the world is yours. No matter which corner of the world you come from.

Key takeaways:

- There are three kinds of creators:
  Actioners (whose golden pill is their hard work), Born Naturals (who get virality/reach/followers because of their natural flair), and Curious Passers-by (who try content creation and then give up when their first three content pieces don't go viral).
- Your natural instinct might be to be in any of these categories. However, if you are a born natural or curious passer-by, you eventually have to become an actioner. That's the holy grail.
- If you are willing to put in the hard work and be consistent, the Creator Economy is yours. No matter which corner of the world you come from.

Chapter 3(c)

How the World Defines
Creators/Influencers

The stories of Gangavva, Shalini and Reesa Teesa are examples of how you can create your own economy in the Creator Economy, no matter what you do or where you come from.

In other words, there are enough and more opportunities for the long tail of small creators who individually may not come with massive millions (or even hundreds of thousands of followers), but their contribution to the Creator Economy brings huge engagement and appeal to their respective audiences.

'Long tail' was originally a term that represents that part of a huge population where occurrences (aka followers as a creator) are slightly distant from the 'head' or central part of the population (the creators with millions of followers).

The creators or influencers are basically divided into four categories,[4] based on the number of followers they have:

(I share some examples of creators too, but don't be surprised if through the power and magic of the creator economy, they have already moved to the next, bigger category :)

- **Nano Creators/Influencers**: With 1000 to 10,000 followers, they are a good fit with a niche yet engaged audience. It reminds me of fitness content creator

Thor Cage, who goes by the handle @thor.cage.9 on Instagram, to share at-home workouts, both with and without equipment. And his strong physique clearly signals that he will soon transition into micro and then a macro creator.

- **Micro Creators/Influencers**: With 10,000-1,00,000 followers, they have the best of both worlds of having a strong following as well as an engaged audience. For me, I love capturing the world with my iPhone. Thus, following @emils.pakarklis is a joy as well as a life lesson.

- **Macro Creators/Influencers**: With a following up to one million, they have an engaged audience already. For example, a manifestation coach I follow is Matt Cook, who shares reels on affirmations, transforming our lives through manifestation, and the power we all have in our minds, all through his aesthetically curated Instagram feed.

- **Mega Creators/Influencers**: With a following of more than one million, they are some of the best recognized faces on the internet. While their popularity ensures that they are in top order for establishing brand awareness or driving sales from a larger community, they come at an astronomical price. For instance, most of us recognize Cristiano Ronaldo—with a cool 637+ million followers on Instagram. Did you know Ronaldo also charges upwards of $3.23 million per post? He is the most followed mega creator on the 'Gram. On YouTube, his channel which he started on 21 August 2024, became the fastest to hit 1 million subscribers—it took him less than 90 minutes. And then he crossed ten million within ten hours. As of early 2025, he was sitting at a whopping 73 million followers!

So even if you're just starting out as a nano creator or are a well-established brand in yourself as a mega creator, this is what the

Creator Economy has enabled—content for all, by all, with no limits or barriers or forms to be filled before entering.

Just will, dedication, and maybe a nudge from someone writing a book about the Creator Economy will get you going.

With this clarity, moving to the next chapter, we will dive deeper into the differences between creators and influencers, explore what this means for collaborators (brands), and outline the steps for anyone starting out to become one.

Key takeaways:

- Broadly, there are four tiers of creators, depending on the size of their following: Nano Creators (<10,000 followers), Micro Creators (10,000–1,00,000 followers), Macro Creators(1,00,000–one million followers), Mega Creators (>one million followers).

- While the number of followers is a critical factor in deciding the money you will make, because brands get more visibility, the importance of quality of that followership cannot be undermined either. Hence, engagement metrics are extremely important while collaborating with creators as the brands are likely to invest more in creators that drive conversations and conversions, and not just a number to display on their page.

- While quantity and quality both create a great leverage, it all starts when you are a nano creator. Trust is the binding factor of the Creator Economy.

- Follower numbers are only, however, the tip of the iceberg that can help start a conversation with a prospective brand. What this means is: If you are creating content that makes your audience trust you and engage with your content through comments, likes and shares (even when you have a 'small' audience), that little audience will create a snowball effect, giving you more followers. Over time, this is the only sustainable and trustworthy way to grow as a creator.

Chapter 3(d)

Creators and Influencers:
Different or Similar?

It was a normal Tuesday morning. I was working at my desk while sipping water from my 'Fat Tuesday' purple sipper when I received a call from a director of a *Fortune* 100 multinational company, who also happens to be a friend.

From a call that lasted forty-five minutes, I want to share the most insightful takeaway from our conversation. And I'm sure you'll agree:

What is the difference between a creator and an influencer? Are they interchangeable terms?

Being in the inside-out of the Creator Economy for so many years now, I come across this question at least once a week.

Interestingly, the lines between how one defines a creator versus an influencer are always burry.

From the early days of the Creator Economy, there have been several well-intentioned demarcation efforts.

In the earlier days, there was a school of thought that impressed upon the idea that if you were creating content 'online first', you'd be a creator, while if you were an offline personality first and an online personality later, you'd be an influencer. Movie stars are an example. So, by that definition,

Jimmy Donaldson, better known as MrBeast, would be a creator and Taylor Swift would be an influencer.

Gradually, an approach emerged that attempted to demarcate creators and influencers on the basis of their follower counts. This was clearly an inaccurate measure on many counts. An offline person who enjoys a relatively good fan following might take very little time to gain the same number of followers as someone like Dudes Perfect or Brent Rivera, who have been creating content for so many years.

Here is how I would think of it in the simplest terms:

A creator is someone who 'creates' original content on social media. They do it specifically by taking care of the intersection of two things: content that they enjoy creating and content that their audience loves consuming.

The content could be anything—personal stories, tips and hacks on a particular topic, comedy, how-to advice, blogging, vlogging, gaming, cooking, literally anything.

Influencer, on the other hand, is someone who through their content (and hence, through their online popularity) has the power to influence their audience's purchasing decisions.

Here's the interesting point that Keith Bendes, a renowned thought leader in influencer marketing and the Creator Economy, highlighted (I'm paraphrasing):

What makes someone a creator or an influencer is not determined by them, but the brand they are collaborating with, and the intent beneath the collaboration.

My interpretation of this is that if a brand is launching a new product and wants to drive a campaign for its awareness, they are collaborating with a creator.

However, if a brand wants to drive 'sales' to their product, they are working with an influencer because they want to track performance metrics (the back end data dashboard of shares, reach, etc., provided to influencer social media accounts) or conversions (number of clicks that converted into 'purchase'), and would want to work with someone who has an established credibility for driving links. Consumers will not differentiate if they are consuming the content of a creator or an influencer, however, for a collaborator (brand), being aware of this distinction makes the biggest difference.

Think of the creator–influencer relationship like this:

1. A creator and an influencer peacefully coexist. They are the different faces of the same coin. The difference is in purpose—driving brand awareness (creator) or performance metrics (influencer).

2. However, the only way to generate trust in an audience and to influence sales is by being a creator consistently. What that means is, if a creator only picks up brand collaborations aimed at driving conversions, the audience will quickly sense that their priority is making money rather than building a genuine connection.

3. Being a consistent creator is what fosters a loyal relationship with the audience. The more a creator develops that trust with their audience, the more a brand trusts them as an influencer (to drive performance and sales) as well as a creator (for brand awareness).

4. Being a creator or being an influencer is not about living in two separate homes. It is rather about getting out of one room in the same home, to another, depending on the intent of the content that is being created.

5. A lot of brands often choose to work with influencers on a long-term basis (after a successful one-off campaign), because performance (especially sales) does not always happen right away. Rather, the audience needs to be exposed to the brand or product multiple times (often through brand awareness—as a creator) before they make the purchase, eventually.[5]

Key takeaways:

- Earlier definition of creators and influencers:
  If you started online first and built an audience, you'd be a creator. If you started offline first and built an audience, you would be an influencer.
- Over time as the Creator Economy flourished, the definitions have evolved into a simpler, more universal approach:
  A creator is someone who creates content. An influencer is someone who influences the decisions of their audience.
- It is the intent of the content they put out, for the brand that they collaborate with, which determines whether they are a creator or an Influencer
- A creator and an influencer are not two different buildings that exist in isolation from each other. They are rather two different rooms in the same apartment, where the same person can enter and exit multiple times.
- An influencer, to influence decisions, has to be a creator as well. If they only pick up brand collaborations to drive sales, the audience will not trust them enough.
- The brand collaborations could be long-term or one-time, based on what the brand is looking for, and what the creator brings on the table, and the amalgamation of the two.

Chapter 3(e)

The Brass Tacks of Being a Creator

As per a Goldman Sachs Report, the Creator Economy could reach half a trillion dollars by 2027.[6]

As of 2023, the Total Addressable Market (TAM) of the Creator Economy is worth $250 billion, with 303 million creators present in the Creator Economy already.[7]

(Note: A report by Adobe states that there are 303 million creators in nine markets comprising the United States, Australia, United Kingdom, Japan, Germany, France, Spain, South Korea and Brazil. You can only imagine how this number extrapolates to the entire world!)

The Goldman Sachs Report goes on to say:

The analysts expect spending on influencer marketing and platform payouts fuelled by the monetization of short-form video platforms via advertising to be the primary growth drivers of the Creator Economy.

Global marketer and bestselling author Gary Vaynerchuk puts it this way: *If you are not crushing it and focusing on the content that you put out on the most important social platforms, you're going to become mute and obsolete in the modern day of doing business.*

That's why organic reach (through a creator or an influencer) is so important because the impression you get when someone comes directly to your page is a much more qualified lead and potentially a more valuable customer than someone you got through an ad buy.[8]

The How of Creator and Influencer Marketing

I know what you are thinking. Facts are good. What would be helpful to you is to understand how it happens.

Let's take a deep dive:

The fundamental rule of marketing states that every customer, before becoming a customer, needs to be aware of the product and made familiar with it at least seven times before they become a customer.[9]

We will understand this further by the Attention Interest Desire Action (AIDA) model and the 95:5 rule, and what they mean for creators, collaborators and customers.

In 1898, E. St. Elmo Lewis developed something called the purchase funnel, which describes the customer's journey from the time they are made aware of the product till the time they eventually make a purchase.

The purchase funnel[10] is very valid in modern day marketing as well, and is often referred to as the AIDA model, which stands for:

A: Attention or Awareness
I: Interest
D: Desire
A: Action

A customer needs to go from capturing attention, sparking interest and invoking desire to have the product in their journey, that will finally lead them to taking action or making a purchase decision.

As per the 95:5 Rule, Professor John Dawes of Ehrenberg-Bass Institute argues that at any point of time only 5 per cent of buyers in the market are ready to buy in the market, while 95 per cent will either buy it later or still need to be convinced over a period of time.[11]

Combine both these models, and here is what it means for the Creator Economy.

Every collaborator (brand) needs to leverage the power of creators, to take care of infusing attention, interest and desire in their 95 per cent customers and new prospects, so that the influencers can provoke 'action' from the 5 per cent.

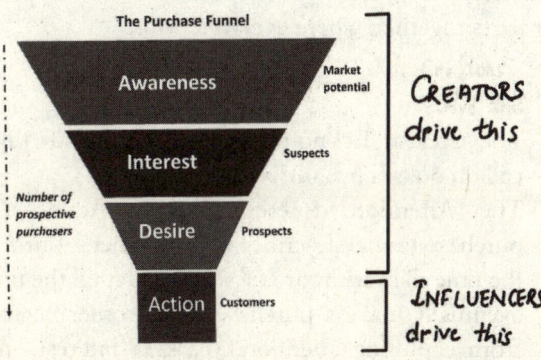

It is also important that collaborators leverage both creators and influencers, and not only influencers. Like we spoke before, creators and influencers are merely the same person living in the same house, just walking across different rooms (from influencer to creator or creator to influencer), based on what the situation demands.

As per a study by Harvard Business Review:[12]

'It may be tempting to turn to influencers when promoting a new product launch…(however the) ROI for influencer posts announcing new products was 30.5 per cent lower than for equivalent posts that were not about new product launches… While short-term ROI can guide short-term decisions, brands should also consider the potential long-term effects of associating with a particular influencer (read: creator). These effects (whether positive or negative) may take time to materialize but can have a substantial impact on a brand's identity.'

The best part is that there's no friction between any of these. A creator can effortlessly choose to become an influencer. An influencer can choose to be a creator. It is fluid. A brand can choose to work with the same person, in a different capacity, either as a creator or an influencer.

Everyone works together to serve the consumer, which is how the Creator Economy functions at its best—keeping all its moving parts together, where everyone wins.

Key takeaways:

- The Creator Economy is going to be worth half a trillion dollars by 2027.
- The Attention, Interest, Desire, Action (AIDA) purchase funnel describes the customer's journey from the time they are aware of the product till the time they eventually make a purchase. A customer needs to go from capturing attention, sparking interest, invoking desire to have the product in their journey, that will finally lead them to taking action.
- As per the 95:5 Rule, at any point in time, only 5 per cent of buyers in the market are ready to buy in the market, while 95 per cent will either buy it later, or still need to be convinced over a period of time.
- Combining both these models, every collaborator (brand) needs to leverage the power of creators to take care of infusing attention, interest and desire in their 95 per cent customers and new prospects, so that the influencers can provoke 'action' from the 5 per cent.
- The best part is: A brand can choose to work with the same person in a different capacity, either as a creator or an influencer.

Chapter 3(f)

The Niches and the Riches of Creators and Influencers

If you want to be a creator, it is akin to learning to play tennis or any sport.

Most people would go to the tennis court and start playing tennis. Alas, that is the last way any professional becomes one.

If you really want to get good at it, you need to understand the grip, stance, swing technique, forehand, backhand, serve, volley and the rules of the game to be a pro at it.

Winning big in the Creator Economy isn't very different. When you know what you do (and what you don't do), you create bigger chances of winning at it.

That is why, before we go on to figure out the journey of becoming an online influencer or a creator, it would be helpful to understand what categories are open to you, and how much of an open landscape you have, to build your territory.

Broadly, all creators and influencers fall into the following niches:

Entertainment: These kinds of creators mainly intend to provide amusement, humour, drama, romance, suspense or some sort of emotional engagement to their audience.

Examples are YouTubers running scripted stories, comedians, mimic artists.

Education: Creators with the intent to teach, simplify or explain complex topics to their audience, usually out of their expertise and experience. Examples are online teachers, course creators, business people sharing their expertise through content creation.

Edutainment: Creators who combine education with fun, at the intersection of both the above categories. Examples include teachers who have their students engage in fun activities to demonstrate a concept, then guide them on how to do it.

Infotainment: Creators who do not share or create new content but curate it and share it with their audience, often in an entertaining way. Examples are news channels reporting news in a way that the audience relates to.

While the sub-categories may be infinite, most creators fall into one or more of these categories—whether it is photographers, vloggers, bloggers, podcasters, travel and tourism creators, fashionistas, DIY crafts, unboxing videos, tech teachers, finance or sustainability experts.

The list literally goes on and on and on.

You could go on to invent your own category and be a star at it.

With that, let's get down to business, of how you become a creator in the first place.

Key takeaways:

- There are four different categories of creators/ influencers:

    Entertainment: Creators that provide some sort of emotional engagement to their audience in the form of amusement, humour, drama, romance, suspense, or any sort of emotional engagement to their audience.

Education: Creators teaching complex topics or even educational ones to their audience, usually out of their expertise and experience.

Edutainment: Creators who combine education with entertainment, at the intersection of both the above categories.

Infotainment: Creators who create content that educate their audience, often in a way that is amusing and not directly a teacher-student kind of conversation.

- You could also go out and create your own category. After all, the Creator Economy is where you could literally 'create your own economy'.

Chapter 3(g)

How Do I Become a Creator?

To answer the question that most of you might be wondering right now—what does it take to become an influencer or a creator?

Here are some valuable insights that might help you:

1. Start creating

Experiment. Do whatever you are drawn towards and what you like. If you like recording videos, open your phone and start putting them out on Instagram or TikTok or YouTube shorts. If you like telling longer visual stories, start putting out longer YouTube videos. If you like writing, X (formerly Twitter) and LinkedIn are potential goldmines. If you are a podcast or Audible person, start creating podcasts.

There are almost zero barriers to entry on any platform. You just have to start.

At the risk of sounding cliche, remember what Jim Rohn said, 'Start from wherever you are and with whatever you've got.'

2. Engage with your audience

The common thread amongst creators who develop a cult is that they engage with their audience consistently. And over time, it becomes a community that serves you.

Engaging could be as simple as responding to Direct Messages (DMs) or comments, hosting live Ask Me Anything (AMA) sessions, creating polls for audience feedback or insights, or holding giveaways for lucky winners in exchange for interacting with the creator.

When a creator, no matter how small or big, engages with their audience, it shows they care about them. It is the online equivalent of Taylor Swift shaking hands with a fan in the middle of a performance. She even travelled to Ohio once to attend a fan's wedding, because she received the invitation in her mail. This reminds me of Ed Sheeran's India tour of March 2023, where he stayed in the country for four to five days before the concert, met a lot of creators, gave lots of interviews, ate local food, danced to a bhangra version of 'Shape of You'.

After all, they are Taylor Swift and Ed Sheeran. They don't have to do all of these. You and I will still flock to their concerts and shout out loud 'It's me, hi!' or 'Darling you look perfect tonight'. However, the reason that they take time off their busy schedules and figure out a way to connect with their audience is the very reason we all love them so much. Because they care.

It's something every creator must follow.

However, when we talk of practicality for people who are starting out into the Creator Economy, most people start with zero to little audience. The best way, then, to get to engage with your audience is to comment on posts of people who have your ideal audience. The secret sauce is, making those comments real and meaningful so that people who read them can't resist visiting your profile to check it out.

If you're becoming a creator focused on fashion styling, comment on posts by other stylists, fashion brands, and influencers who endorse these stylists. If you are sharing your wisdom from the experience you gained from your work life, engage with posts of others who also share their work experience or share actionable content on work life.

With patience, persistence and good content, you will slowly start to build a community you are proud of building, every single day.

3. Analyse data

Funded start-ups that send a weekly update of their business metrics to their Venture Capitalists (VCs) and angel investors tend to perform better than those that don't.

Of course, there are multiple metrics to a start-up success such as product, being at the right place at the right time, promoting it right, and getting the cost right among other things. However, I believe in tracking all of these triumphs, as it clearly shows what's working, what isn't, and how to make the necessary changes.

The same is the case with being a creator.

A running Google sheet updated weekly, tracking metrics such as engagement, impressions, reach, comments, shares, likes, etc., will serve multiple purposes, including:

- Provide valuable insights on your content strategy— should you post more often or less, if you are into videos. should they be longer or shorter, if you are into text or blogs, should they be longer or shorter.
- Insights from platforms also reveal your audience's location, gender, age groups, and designation (on LinkedIn). These are valuable metrics for determining whether you are reaching the right audience.

4. Listen to your audience

One way audiences tell you what they love and what they don't is, of course, through data. The other way is putting your ear to the ground and listening carefully to your social chatter.

What comments do they leave on your posts?

What comments do they leave on posts of other creators in your niche?

Which story was shared the most?

What is something you thought would go viral but did not even see the light of an average post?

Top movie directors, entrepreneurs, and inventors all begin with an idea and then conduct customer research to ensure they address all the pain points of their audience.

5. Be innovative

Experiment with new things. For a change, put out content that you think can challenge you, even if you are not sure how the audience might receive it.

Get out of your own way and give wings to your creativity.

Being differentiated is the secret sauce to being creative, especially if you are on more than one platform.

All social platforms have a character to them, such as LinkedIn for professional content and Instagram for creative storytelling.

Someone who follows your content expects Instagram to showcase your creative flair and LinkedIn to highlight your professional achievements. While many might argue that the distinction between the two platforms is gradually fading, I'd say that applies to the formats (videos, photos, carousels, etc.), not the core content proposition.

Even if you repost a tweet as a screenshot on LinkedIn, can you make it relevant and relatable in the caption? Can you take a snippet of a podcast conversation and post it on Instagram as a meme? Can you take a picture of your Behind-the-Scene (BTS) process and post it as a story on Instagram? And then, can you go on to share one of the responses to that story as another story or a post on another platform?

Your content is an extension of your expression. Thus, it would only be prudent to be mindful of what you'd like to present for the world to see.

6. Be consistent

Consistency does not mean posting daily.

It simply means posting consistently at regular intervals, no matter if it's snowing, raining, or the sun is shining.

If you create long-form videos, maybe start with one or two a week. If you create shorts or reels, four to six a week is a good number to start with. The same is the case with LinkedIn. A newsletter is good for weekly frequency.

You pick the day of the week. And then post content invariably on that day. Even if it is not perfect.

And to help you consistently aim for near-perfection, here's another point:

7. Create a process around your content creation

If you would have to schedule a meeting with your manager's manager or anyone at a higher rung in the organization, you would have to look for a time in their calendars.

Because important people have their days, weeks and sometimes months scheduled down to a T.

Which is the exact status and seriousness you ought to give to your creation process as well.

Can you note down ideas on a weekend?

Then create the first draft of all of them together, in one go. Then edit them together, in another sitting. For an entire week. Or a fortnight, if you wish to.

There are creators who keep an entire day on their calendar empty to shoot an entire week's content—long form and short form. Writers write for all their clients at one go, go for long walks, and then edit that content in two to three sittings in small intervals.

This isn't just true for those who start; we also mentioned Ed Sheeran earlier in the book, who follows the same exact process. The difference is that using one of the world's top singers as an example of 'process' helps people relate, showing they're not cut from a different cloth. It was the fifth song of the day, during months when he'd compose music daily from 9 to 5, and only one song from that entire month might be deemed 'good enough' It was all part of the process.

Is it going to be easy if you set a process?

No practice routine was easy even for Michael Jordan. But the fact that he showed up and put in the work, even on days when he didn't feel like it, is what made him what he is. Today, people spend fortunes on getting his Air Jordans, while most people wearing the shoes can't name any of Jordan's teammates.

There is pain in the process. So is there a prize.

8. Have fun in the process

Here is where the secret sauce lies: It is virtually possible to copy any big creator's process—whether it is creating productivity videos like Ali Abdaal, sharing insightful observations on work life like Adam Grant, or making serious stuff look a little less serious like Dan Pink. Ask AI for prompts to generate similar content ideas, and you will have a flood of inspiration to create endless content.

However, if it is something you don't enjoy, no artificial or human intelligence can help you build an audience and become an influencer.

The best creators and influencers enjoy their process of creation and would do that even if they were not paid.

Shaan Puri ✓
@ShaanVP

My career strategy: Get paid huge sums of money to do something I'd gladly do for free

Which is why having fun in the process is very important.

Also, becoming a creator and eventually making tons of money is much like starting your own business—it requires passion, hard work, patience and infinite dedication which can exist only if it is something you enjoy.

9. Rinse and repeat

As a creator, there may be times when your video gets half-a-million views with just 20,000 subscribers/followers. Other times, you would be standing at 2 million followers and still struggling to get 50,000 views.

The only way to get going is to go back to the above pointers and figure out where it is that you need to tweak things. The basics are the boss. An intelligent influencer would never forget that.

...

However, when you do become an influencer, I think it is wise to know that it is not always a bed of roses. There are thorns, and it is only pragmatic to expect that everyone has them.

For example, along with fame and fortune, follow critics and complications. A lot of well-meaning creators have haters and must deal with complications they did not sign up for. At times, something as big as their YouTube channels being hacked. Sometimes, it impacts the creator's self-worth far beyond the lifespan of the criticism itself.

Also, since a lot of your success is dependent on numbers, sometimes a lot of artistic, individualistic creators tend to kill their art and instincts just to fit into the cacophony of 'growth', which, in my humble opinion, is a recipe for disaster. Who are you if you are not yourself?

As a corporate employee, you're also entitled to take some time off. But as a self-employed creator, even when you are on a vacation, you are either creating content or consuming statistics of your creation. So, it is a matter of willpower and active choices to be on a vacation instead of letting content consume you.

We will discuss real, actionable ways to cope with the cons of being a creator in chapter 4(e) Mental Health for Creators.

But in my vast experience of more than two decades in multiple fields of work, I know of no job that does not come with its cons. In all of those jobs as well, there are people who are making their mark and being truly successful, because they chose to plunge with the pros instead of getting crumbled by the cons. The world is your oyster only if you choose it to be. More so, in the Creator Economy world.

. . .

Being an influencer is as good as becoming consistently profitable in a bootstrapped company. Looks shiny and 'worthy of copying' for everyone and to everyone.

It is not as smooth as it looks and is exactly like a duck paddling in water—smooth to everyone, with lots of effort going on underneath the surface.

If you're like a duck, gliding smoothly on the surface while paddling hard underneath, being an influencer might seem 'easy'—if you nail these basics.

And if you're ready to step into the influencer market, it's time to get real about the platforms and what they mean to you—whether you're an innovator, a creator, a brand, or a consumer.

Key takeaways:

The step-by-step process of becoming a creator from scratch (reverse engineer any creator's content journey, and you will find almost the same process):

- Start creating: Start creating content on what you truly enjoy doing—whether it is videos, text, graphics or even podcasting. The barriers are nil. The only thing you need is intent.
- Engage with your audience: The best creators engage with their audience even after crossing millions of followers. It is a slow yet steady path of growing as a creator. After all, business is all about relationships.

- Analyse data: A running Google sheet updated with all metrics of the platform you create content on. A data report is consumer behaviour out loud in front of our eyes. While we must not blindly follow data all the time, 95 per cent of the time it still holds the answer.

- Listen to your audience: Comments on your content, on competitors' content, likes, and even the posts you thought would go viral but didn't—these are valuable insights from the audience. If used wisely, they can make fortunes for every creator because they are essentially 'building in public'.

- Be innovative: The audience doesn't doesn't say so but it loves how creators experiment. Even if you repost your content from one platform to another, how can you be innovative with respect to the audience of the platform the content is now being posted on? Your content is an extension of your expression. Use it well.

- Be consistent: Show up at a regular intervals. If not daily, post something new weekly, monthly or fortnightly. The audience expects you and that anticipation builds trust.

- Create a process around your creation: We are all creatures of habit. Even the most creative people have a process to just show up at a time, which is when creativity happens. If you only wait for inspiration to strike, you might keep waiting for the longest time.

- Have fun in the process: The audience sees through things when you are forcing something and are not genuinely enjoying it. That Does not mean it won't be hard. It will be. But you choose your difficulty: Creating content on what you love or simply following the crowd.

- Rinse and repeat: Stay in the game. And each time you hit a bump on the road, go back to the basics. When nothing else works, basics do. Being a creator isn't as smooth as it looks, but if done well, with the right intent and process, winning is inevitable.

Chapter 3(h)

Small Screen to Big Screen, and Big Screen to Small

A twenty-one-year-old radio jockey in the suburbs of Mumbai was dissatisfied with her career. After interning at a popular radio station for a year, she had landed her first show. However, the show was a commercial failure.

Thus, at the intersection of her lack of joy in radio and lack of commercial success, she asked her parents if she could take a year to start making videos.

Guess what her parents said?

'Take two.'

In a way, they wheeled her into believing she had all the support, which she, of course, did.

Almost a decade later, we know that former radio jockey as YouTuber Prajakta Koli, popularly known as MostlySane. Through her fun yet authentic style of creating content, she has not only amassed a following of 8.3 million on Instagram, and 7.1 million on YouTube as of early-2025, she also boasts of the following achievements:

- In 2019, the then YouTube CEO (late) Susan Wojcicki selected Prajakta Koli's 'Real Talk Tuesday' series as the interview platform for her first-ever interaction with an Indian YouTuber.

- In the years that followed, she has interviewed several Indian and international artists, including Brie Larson, Samuel L. Jackson, Sadhguru, Priyanka Chopra, Adam Sandler and Jennifer Aniston.
- Prajakta represented India at *The Call To Unite* event, which started on 1 May 2020 and featured Oprah Winfrey, Julia Roberts, Eva Longoria, Deepak Chopra, Alanis Morissette, Quincy Jones and Mandy Moore, among others.
- On 7 June 2020, Koli was part of the virtual graduation ceremony, Dear Class of 2020, headlined by former President Barack Obama and former First Lady Michelle Obama which was live streamed via YouTube Originals.
- In January 2022, she was appointed UNDP India's first Youth Climate Champion.
- A year later, she was one of the six content creators invited globally for the World Economic Forum in Davos.
- Another year later, in 2024, Prajakta was the only Indian creator among 'celebrities' selected by the International Olympic Committee to participate in a 10K marathon in Paris 2024 Olympics.[13]
- She also published her debut novel in January 2025, and quicker than you and I could think, it hit the bestseller list.

As you can see, Koli boasts of a track record as a creator that comes only with relentless consistency, hard work and staying true to the process.

What has unfolded for her in the process is how she landed opportunities in Bollywood movies, thanks to her dedicated following, whom she lovingly calls 'Dumdums'.

She worked in *Jugg Jugg Jiyo*, a mass entertainment movie produced by Dharma Productions, one of the largest movie production companies in India. She also bagged a significant role in the movie *Neeyat*, starring Vidya Balan.

Besides movies, she has also played the lead character in the Netflix series *Mismatched*, opposite Rohit Sarraf.

Not just Prajakta, but many Indian and global content creators have gone on to star in mainstream movies. For example, comedian Anubhav Singh Bassi played a pivotal role in the movie *Tu Jhoothi Main Makkar* as Ranbir Kapoor's best friend.

If that is not enough inspiration, another huge YouTuber named Bhuvan Bam had his own OTT series called *Taaza Khabar* that received massive appreciation from his fans.

Trot around the globe, and the trend is massive.

Charli D'Amelio, who has 155 million followers on TikTok (and is the second most followed person on the platform) was given a run in 2020's *StarDog* and *TurboCat*. She has since made a cameo appearance in *The Simpsons*, and is set to feature in the upcoming film, *Home School*.

Another social media star, Andrew Byron Bachelor, better known as King Bach, was once the most followed person on Vine. His humour and six-seconds-long content helped capture the attention of 11.3 million people. He later went on to star in 2016 comedy movies *Meet the Blacks* and *Fifty Shades of Black* and the horror-comedy *Babysitter* a year later.

But the shift isn't only from the small screen to the big screen. A reverse shift is also happening at the same time. Lines are blurring.

Movie stars, sports personalities, singers, musicians, entrepreneurs—all the rich and famous people whose fame comes from outside social media—are also leveraging these platforms to directly connect with fans, share their real side way from the media-tailored industry, or to build a distribution.

A classic example is Victoria Beckham, also known as Posh Spice. In the 1990s, Posh was a member of the immensely popular all-female group the Spice Girls. Through multiple solo releases as well as albums and a thriving career as a singer, in 2008, she launched her own fashion label. As of now, Posh keeps her fans and followers updated on her latest offerings, through her Instagram account that boasts of 33 million followers. The best part is, her posts are not only about business. She has also chosen to share glimpses of her personal life, which, I believe, makes her as well as the brand very real and relatable.

Or let's look at the FIFA World Cup winning champion Lionel Messi. He does not have to be a part of the Creator Economy, but he chooses to, for what it's worth. Along with sharing his football life and brand endorsements, Messi also tries to make it real in his own way, to his 500 million followers.

Back home in India, it reminds me of one of the youngest billionaires of the country Nikhil Kamath, who runs several companies, along with Zerodha, with his elder brother Nithin. He has seen the pinnacle of success, fame and fortune. Nikhil was the youngest billionaire in India, according to *Forbes* 2024 list.[14]

However, early in 2023, he decided to launch his own podcast. It is unlike any other podcast you have seen or heard of. A group of smart people from a niche, gathered around a table, chatting for 2-3 hours—defying every conventional podcast format that existed until then. His goal was certainly to quantify quality over quantity, which is why he barely publishes one podcast a month.

Fun Fact: When Nikhil Kamath turned up at the Nas Daily Creator Summit, he was recognized as the 'man who creates epic podcasts' and not for all the (bigger and perhaps more noteworthy) achievements he already has in his kitty.

Key takeaways:

- If there is a spark in you towards a particular niche of content creation, just go for it. Give it a chance. Give yourself a chance.
- The percolation of creators from small screens to big screens is a massive leap for the Creator Economy. And the heights where it is supposed to go.
- Also, big names from the top of their industries, who have risen to prominence through their offline work, are now also becoming creators. These are people with an abundance of money, fame, success, you name it. The Creator Economy is nothing less than a magnet, I'd say.

Chapter 3(i)

Bringing the 5Cs of the Creator Economy Together

Now that we have understood the ins and outs of the Creator Economy, it is time to dive deeper into each pillar and explore where you stand and where the opportunities lie for you.

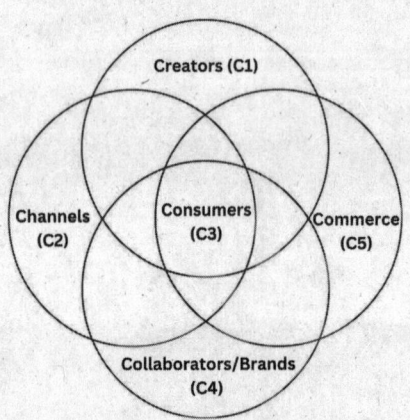

The 5Cs of the Creator Economy

As you can see in the picture, the audience or the consumer is at the centre stage, with creators, brands, innovators and commerce being the four pillars.

In this book, we have been talking from the point of view of the creator because the economy is literally called the Creator Economy, and the remaining four pillars govern how the creator interacts with the other parts of the ecosystem—of how the creator is making money, where the brands are coming in and how the ecosystem functions for the tech that is enabling all of this, with the audience never leaving the centre stage.

So, let's go:

Creators (C1):

Find a voice on a platform that you are the best at. Double down on it. Rinse and repeat.

James Clear, the author of Atomic Habits, is a classic example. He started writing his 3-2-1 newsletter in November 2012 with zero subscribers. (Yes, James Clear also started at zero like the rest of us.) In November 2015, when he grew to 2,00,000 followers, he struck a deal with Penguin Random House for a book, which the world would come to know as Atomic Habits.

Atomic Habits was released early in the year 2018, and for six years after that, all that James did was consistently write his newsletter. As of January 2024, he has over 3 million subscribers to his newsletter.

At this point, in February 2024, James went on to a different vertical and launched his app called 'Atoms', taking all the principles from his book, and being a daily guide to help people form better habits.

Thirteen years after working relentlessly on one platform.

He has social pages on Instagram, LinkedIn and Twitter, but they are mainly reposts of his newsletter of Atomic Habits. No reels, threads or long form videos. Just the same thing, over and over again. As a matter of fact, he asks his assistant to change his social media password every Monday, and then she hands it over to him on every Saturday. No torment of choice to enforce rigidity of discipline. He just makes it impossible for himself to do 'more'.

To paraphrase none other than James Clear, 'Do less, but better'.

Channels (C2):

The platforms that disrupted the marketplace didn't start with the intention of doing so.

They simply identified a small market gap, listened to customer feedback, innovated, and iterated. And, day by day, they sparked a movement and caused massive disruption.

Facebook innovated way faster than Orkut, and protected people's privacy; hence, it rose to three billion monthly active users.

Instagram made photo-sharing instant and sharing details of your life in stories very easy.

Twitter (now X) in its former days allowed people to interact with each other in mini sentences (initially 140 characters, later 280 characters), enabling quick exchange of messages.

WhatsApp was invented by Jan Koum in 2009, when he was travelling internationally and did not have the money to call his parents back home. As of today, the entire world can make international phone calls with just an internet connection and zero charges.

Any other platform that you use today addresses your needs of connection in ways no other platform has, which is why it is thriving.

However, on the other hand, there are multiple examples of organizations that did not grow at the pace their competitors grew and ultimately folded. Blackberry, for example, lost the battle when Apple and Samsung smartphones came to the forefront. Fundamentally, the company's mistakes were linked to an excessive focus on enterprise over consumer tastes and preferences, to an operating system that nobody was building apps for.[15] In my opinion, it serves as an example for all channels and innovators to learn from: with the passage of time, it's crucial to adapt to the changing tide. Which is why Apple thrived, Netflix thrived despite being laughed out of Blockbuster's office[16] and which is why trees that bend the most yield the most fruits.

Thus, as an innovator, it is important to bring platforms that address gaps for the audience and help them connect better.

An excellent example of this, where innovators could draw a leaf from, is Kajabi.

Kajabi is a SaaS (Software as a Service) company that develops a platform for creators to create, market and sell digital content.

The platform was launched by Kenny Rueter, a software engineer in Irvine, California, after he faced difficulty trying to monetize a how-to video on YouTube. What started as a project to solve his son's problems, is now a unicorn with a $2 billion valuation as of 2024.

Among the many problems that Kajabi solves, here are the most important solutions they offer:

1. It has integrated various softwares that creators need to run their digital businesses, such as:
   • The ability to send automated messages. It takes away the need to apply a lot of automatic zaps that connect multiple platforms together.
   • The ability to integrate Shopify to enable people to 'buy'.
   • The ability to create a website within its ecosystem. Goodbye WordPress or any other web designing tool.
   • The ability to send emails to its users as per the desired time of the creator. It takes away the need for Mailchimp or ConvertKit or Sendlane or any other email marketing tool.

- The ability to create course memberships for the people who bought the creator's course, taking away the need for course designing platforms and facilitating all of the above integrations.
- The ability to create communities of the audience and manage them, which is a relaxing thing considering all the audience is now in one place!
- Not to miss, the creator(s) or their team must master one platform very well, instead of hanging around on different platforms and at different places.

Fun fact: With a user base of over 60,000 creators, Kajabi has paid out over $5 billion since its inception.

2. It also allows users to receive payments in any currency and in multiple currencies.
3. Users can see analytics of all the courses, content and communities they create—which is gold for any creator.
4. Above all, there is no transaction fee, no matter which product you sign up for. There is a blanket monthly/annual platform cost and the creator is allowed to keep 100 per cent of the revenue they make.

If there's a revolution that has truly blown my mind, it's Kajabi. It alleviated the pain of so many creators and likely prompted all the integrating platforms to rethink their strategies.

Of course, all these platforms are still relevant individually, but for a course creator whose biggest headache was to make sure all integrations are running and no screw in the machinery is broken, Kajabi is an angel without disguise.

Consumer/Community (C3):

The Consumer is the ultimate driver of the Creator Economy. Consumers seek content that informs, entertains, or inspires. Unlike traditional media audiences, today's consumer communities are more interactive, often engaging directly with creators through comments, shares and direct messages.

Having said the above, let me be very practical to start with:

I can't tell you where to go or which platform to spend your time on. No one can. But what I can tell you is we human beings do not have time to talk to our friends while our screen time is most of our waking hours. Clearly not the most encouraging signs of our times.

As much as 63 per cent of people on social media report feeling lonely, 40 per cent feel anxious or depressed after using it, and 60 per cent feel the need to take a break from it.[17]

As a matter of fact, social media consumption is also linked to higher rates of anxiety, inadequacy about your life or appearance, FOMO (fear of missing out), isolation, depression and poor sleep quality.

How you should limit your social media consumption is based on two pillars: extrinsic and intrinsic.

Extrinsic methods are what you know already, but for revision:[18]

1. Set blockers on apps and phone.
2. Let that password be with someone else but not you.
3. Schedule your Wi-Fi to shut down at specific times of the day.
4. No phone first thing in the morning or last thing before sleeping.
5. Leave your phone outside the bedroom before sleeping.

    The list is endless.

All of these work to an extent; however, if we are smart, we can also figure a way out to surpass our self-created barriers and consume more of social media.

Which brings us to intrinsic motivation.

Content consumption has filled a void inside us which was not a void in the first place. Now, we never get bored. However, it is boredom that brings out the best in us.

What helps deal with incessant social media consumption is having something to look forward to. Something that pushes your boundaries.

That could be a project at work, or something that you enjoy outside of work.

For example, if you go out and play tennis twice a week on the weekends, working with a coach would improve accountability. It would also help you look forward to the game, identify your blind spots, and consistently improve—without ever forcing yourself or beating yourself up for not being as good as Roger Federer or Novak Djokovic.

It could be a passion project that you can start with your job or take up that venture you have been dreaming about for years.

We often tend to have no time for things that drain our energy whereas our screen time shows tens of hours every week spent on social media.

Finding something to look forward to in your day is where you find the balance.

Collaborators (C4):

This is a golden opportunity for Collaborators or brands to capitalize the most where their ideal audience lies.

If you are a skincare or a beauty brand, no other platform is better than Instagram. It's a platform where the audience is more likely to buy such products.

If you have a learning product, LinkedIn or X (formerly Twitter) might be great places to spark that chatter.

Before reaching out to an influencer and choosing their platform, a brand must first be clear on the desired output from the influencer marketing campaign. Only then should they select the platform, followed by the creator.

This follows Simon Sinek's golden circle of 'Start with Why'

For brands, here is what the golden circle looks like:

Why: The result they are looking for from the campaign— brand recall (think of this as the 95 per cent of the Attention/ Interest/Desire) or drive action (the sales or conversions).

How: Platform of choice or media mix by the brand—Instagram, TikTok, YouTube, Facebook, etc.

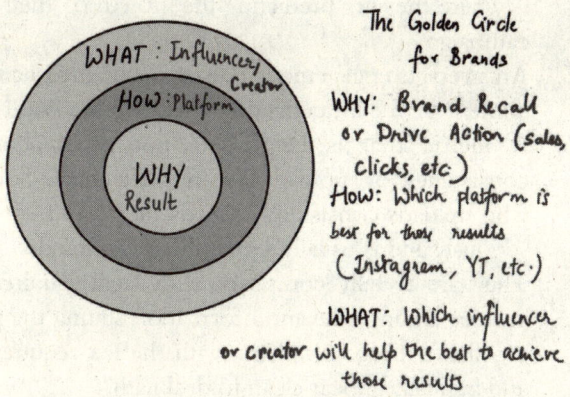

The Golden Circle for Brands

WHY: Brand Recall or Drive Action (sales, clicks, etc.)

How: Which platform is best for those results (Instagram, YT, etc.)

WHAT: Which influencer or creator will help the best to achieve those results

What: Creator or influencer on that platform to be decided by the brand.

Some golden nuggets for brands to monitor:

1. The right influencer matters the most.
    For example, if you want to promote a new launch by Louis Vuitton, it is best to work with an influencer who creates luxury content (even if they have under 1,00,000 followers) instead of working with someone who creates videos of flea markets (even if they have over one million followers).
    The right audience from a smaller sample is always more useful than window shoppers from an irrelevant cohort for the brand.
2. The influencer should have grown their audience organically, and certainly not purchased followers.
3. Comments on former posts of the influencer should be by genuine accounts and not by bots and fake accounts.

4. A data-driven brand will also analyse statistics from the influencer's previous brand collaborations compared to their organic posts and observe the differences. This is where they are predicting the growth of their brand campaign.
5. An average engagement rate is maintained across all content of the influencer. 1-5 per cent is a good norm.
6. A metric that is helpful, if not essential, is the consistency of uploads by the influencer. Someone who uploads consistently signals they take their brand seriously and is usually a green flag for brands.
7. They are usually compliant with legal requirements, such as adding relevant information stating the post is a collaboration, complying with the tax requirements, and basically appear clean to deal with.

With start-ups getting funded incessantly, a lot of money is invested on performance marketing. Sometimes, this leads to incessant brand collaborations without the right research. Eventually it hurts the brand's sales as well as its trust with the customers.

Checking all these boxes prevents exactly that.

After all, the wrong business partnerships can lead to stress, frustration and prolonged insomnia. On the other hand, the right business partnerships are often the greatest recipe for a peaceful night's sleep.

Commerce (C5):

In past centuries, wars were waged by nations vying for control over territories and people. Online wars are fought by platforms deploying the smartest people and fighting to build their cult audience and monetize them.

Commerce involves converting content and influence into revenue streams. This can be achieved not only through ad revenues, but also through sponsored content, merchandise sales, online courses and more. The beauty of the Creator

Economy lies in its scalability; creators can start small and gradually expand their income streams.

The Amazon Affiliate Programme, which started as early as 1996, allows people to share and market any product on Amazon, and they get to make a commission between 1–10 per cent of the price of the product.

On the other hand, Walmart, which is considered one of the largest retail chains globally, launched a creator programme in 2022, that allows users to create affiliate links of their products, build an online storefront, and make money through commissions, while at the same time allowing them to track the performance of their sales.

The scale of Walmart also brings to surface the magic of Open Network for Digital Commerce (ONDC), which is an initiative by the Government of India to transform the digital commerce ecosystem, specifically for Small and Medium Enterprises (SMEs). Set up in 2021, ONDC creates a fair and open digital commerce network to empower SMEs. These SMEs are thus able to reach a broader customer base and engage in healthy competition instead of having no chance against monopolistic markets. Needless to say, it also comes with the advantage of lower operating costs thus reducing costs to the sellers as well as the buyers.[19]

Another company that is making waves is Patreon, known for its robust support of creators. Fans of creators' videos, art, or writing sign up as 'patreons,' supporting them through monthly subscriptions or per-post pledges. With the intent of not growing the fan base but supporting the existing fan base, Patreon connects true fans to the creator and creates an ecosystem for the former to support the latter.

This trend of having good customer experience and then going on to leverage the audience to build commerce is not new. With the massive success of WhatsApp since its inception in 2009, the company launched WhatsApp Business, where business owners can create a dedicated business profile, and have automated conversations with the users, manage data, create product catalogues, and also offer a business API that integrates WhatsApp Business functionalities to existing customer relationships management tools of the businesses.

These are a few examples, but the scope of growth of platforms—both online and offline (by venturing online like Walmart) are limitless.

The onus on the platforms is to build something that the audience would like to jam on, which is what we discovered as an innovator.

...

The best part of the Creator Economy is that when even one pillar builds itself up, it creates potential for all the other pillars to follow suit. It is the opposite of Tall Poppy Syndrome.

When we are in an economy that is only building everyone up, now is the time to talk about the thing that is the evidence of building: Monetization.

Key takeaways:

Here is what the Creator Economy means for you, for each of the five moving parts:

Creator:

- Find a voice on the platform you are the best at. However, it would be helpful to work on a platform where you are best suited to work hard.
- Your identity + the place where you would enjoy = the right creator in place.
- As James Clear, author of the multimillion bestseller Atomic Habits, says, 'Do less, but better.'

Channel:

- A good channel thrives when it does not intend to make huge promises. Instead, it identifies a market gap, connects with the right audience, and, after enduring its share of setbacks, emerges as a disruptive force in the marketplace

Consumer:

- Consumer/communities are folks like you and me—we consume content.
- Going against the norm so far, I won't tell you what to consume and where to spend your time.
- However, what I would urge you to think is if all the time you spend on social media is worth it. Putting some time away to waste is good, even healthy if I might say, but doing it as a lifestyle is often a curse, as even data has shown.
- Maybe a healthy, strong life outside of social media will create a healthy life with social media?

Collaborator (Brand):

- The success of the brand promotion you collaborate on with creators depends on the platform you work on.
- An ideal brand follows the sequence of: Why, How and What (in that order) on every brand campaign, for the best results. It is equivalent to doing the due diligence an investor does before they put their money into a company.

Commerce:

- As a creator grows, the avenues to monetize grow, too. They can not only make money from brand collaborations (C4) but from multiple other avenues as well—such as affiliate income, creating their own merchandise products, courses, or even showing up at offline events. The possibilities are literally endless, because this is how the Creator Economy helps you Create Your Own Economy.

Chapter 4

My Money Don't Jiggle Jiggle, It Folds—in the Creator Economy

I carry six racquets in my squash bag.

Of these, only two are functional.

What about the remaining four?

Not only do I love them love them too much to let them go, I think each of these racquets reminds me of my journey of playing and loving the sport of squash.

Not just my squash racquets—I still have my military uniform with me, even though it's been over nineteen years since I left the service.

If you have not yet judged me so far, let me help you—it's perfectly normal to feel that I am not being rational with my choices, probably more emotional than rational?

I'd rather put it differently.

I am mostly rational about life, except for things that have defined a part of me in the past.

In other words, I am not Ross from the popular sitcom *Friends*, I identify as Joey.

Joey, the most fun character in FRIENDS, is the coolest one of them all, a darling friend, but also has a quirky side to him.

In one of the episodes, he is so attached to his soft toy penguin, Hugsy, that he is reluctant to allow his friend Rachel to take it away for her daughter Emma. Even though they live in the same apartment.

That is Joey, my friend. The friend you can bank on. The most loyal friend you could ever find. The friend for whom his friends matter the most.

But so does Hugsy.

I also see a bit of Chandler in me.

He has a knack for looking for something funny and sarcastic in every situation. You can't help but laugh when you are around Chandler, even when the situation is super difficult.

At a deeper level, it is more motivating than learning from a motivational speaker.

Chander 'lives' the motivated life, instead of preaching it.

So, here it is, friends, I am somewhat Joey and somewhat Chandler as a person.

But wait.

Why are we speaking about characters from *Friends* here?

Because there is a little bit of one or more *Friends* in each one of us.

You see, my friend, *Friends* didn't enjoy a successful ten-year run because its characters were heroes with capes, swords, and bombs saving cities from destruction. It thrived because every character was beautifully flawed.

Four of the six main characters lived in neighbouring apartments, forming each other's strongest support system, especially when their flaws led them through their darkest moments.

It is the flaws we relate to the most—from one of the most popular sitcoms made in history.

The best part—it was all fun.

Ross and Rachel going on a whirlwind of uncertainties yet being good friends—fun.

Monica being the typical Type A person—fun.

Chandler being the perfect guy friend to Joey and the perfect husband to Monica while having fun in every word that came out of his mouth—fun.

Phoebe being flaky, having the weirdest (yet often correct) opinions and not caring an inch about others before being cardinally honest—fun.

Joey being the best host, best friend, hosting ducks, chickens, chicks (if you know you know), friends without apartments, taking care of them effortlessly—fun.

Its blend of flaws and fun is what made *Friends* one of the most beloved sitcoms ever, even over twenty years after its final season aired.

It not only gave a phenomenal career to the makers and the actors of the show, it created an economy of its own.

Let's dive deep into how:

Consumers:

I am a Gen-X guy who spent the prime years of my youth (age 15–25) watching *Friends* when it was being aired (1994–2004).

Truth be told, I still love it equally. Even more, perhaps, now that I know that the world is made up of flawed people. But here is the fun part: Millennials and Gen Z love the show in equal measure. As much as I would not have expected it, I am glad they do.

It is like a warm hug from another miserable friend who does not judge you for your screw-ups in life and shares their own screw-ups as well.

My son is sixteen and he loves the show as well.

Collaborators (Brands):

Because of the huge popularity, a lot of brands were integrated into the show. Be it as little as wearing Nike sweatshirts or consuming Coke or 7Up, or Chandler playing the game Ms Pac-Man, or as huge as Rachel working at Ralph Lauren.

Fun Fact: Ralph Lauren himself appeared in episode eight of season six, highlighting how brands and creators thrive by standing on each other's shoulders.

It is the best array of multiple case studies of a brand collaborating with content that is already loved and adored throughout the globe.

Channels (Platforms):

Friends has official YouTube, Facebook and Instagram channels that keep sharing snippets from the show. Still. Not only that, but there are also fan clubs who have specific social media pages for different characters of the show. Heck, there are specific Wikipedia pages for the six lead characters of the show. And separate ones, of course, for the actors who played them.

Apart from that, there are a multitude of non-official *Friends* channels on possibly every social media platform further cementing the show's enduring popularity.

Commerce:

If that was not enough, there is *Friends* merchandise that you can keep with yourself—from mugs stating 'I'm Fine', which was a landmark dialogue by the character Ross, to 'Central Perk' t-shirts, the coffee house where the characters used to hang out together.

There is also a pop-up studio of *Friends* at the Union Square in San Francisco where you can visit, and of course, click your pictures, as I have done myself.

In another world, on the 25th anniversary of the show in 2019, Ralph Lauren released a special *Friends* collection, as did Pottery Barn, that launched a special product line around the theme *Friends*.

...

On that note, I want to bring you to an important point regarding the time at which the show aired.

In chapter 1, we spoke about how YouTube and Facebook started at around the same time in 2005 and sowed the seeds for bringing the Creator Economy into action, which we see today.

Here is the fun fact: *Friends* stopped airing mid-2004. Still, it was the best amalgamation of all five pillars of the Creator Economy in action.

The point I am trying to drive home is this:

The Creator Economy and all its five pillars, when strategically combined while making sure they cater to the central pillar i.e. consumer, almost create products (content, in our case) that are next to miracles. Even before the invention of the Creator Economy, we have the classic example of *Friends*!

Which is what *Friends* stood for.

Which is what the best-case amalgamations (of different pillars—from C1, C2, C3, C4 and C5) in the Creator Economy stand for.

In the various parts of this chapter, we will explore how, individually.

P. S.: Like Joey used to sleep with Hugsy by his side, I used to sleep with my basketball and football next to myself for the longest time. But that's a story for another day.

...

Creator Economy Is the Air We Breathe

The example of *Friends* and how it was (and still is) dominant in all five pillars of the Creator Economy is because this is what the Creator Economy is: omnipresent, omnipotent, omniscient. Okay, I'll stop this omni-language. And jump right into business.

The two most essential elements of the Creator Economy (other than the consumer, of course), are creators and brands.

Unlike movies or sports, the Creator Economy now is not a different business or vertical. The Creator Economy, with its advantages and disadvantages, is the air we breathe.

Whether it is an automobile manufacturer or a food joint or an AI-based start-up or a movie production house or a hyperlocal food delivery company in a small city, the Creator Economy is for everyone, by everyone.

As a matter of fact, 17 per cent of creators are business owners, and 39 per cent aspire to become one, eventually.[1] While only more than a quarter (26 per cent) of creators are universally motivated by money, there is more inclination to make content creation a full-time job, with its freedom of expression, control over your time and the infinite opportunities and possibilities it adds up to.

The fact that YouTube shares almost half (45 per cent) of the revenues from ad spends with its creators is another reason to make money that doesn't just jiggle jiggle, but folds.

For every ad that runs on a specific channel, YouTube takes a 55 per cent cut of what the advertiser pays for the placement. The creator gets the remaining 45 per cent. Metrics like cost per mille (CPM) and cost per click (CPC) and the region make the numbers differ, but the answer is more or less the same: go make some money, you creative creator!

...

All of these numbers are a positive sign of the growing potential to become a creator.

When a creator transitions into a full-time businessperson, they also open doors for others to build their own businesses—video editors, graphic designers, sound editors, writers, operators, chiefs of staff, social media managers, creator managers, content curators—the list is truly endless.

A creator that makes money has a ripple effect of creating full-time and part-time employment for many other people.

It truly inspires others to pursue a path as creators.

Imagine how many people went on to become creators because they were fascinated by MrBeast, who also featured on the '100 Most Influential People of 2023' list.[2]

Or how many people focused on performing in rock concerts as a legit dream, instead of getting a job.

Don't get me wrong. There is nothing wrong with getting a job. I am not a creator nor do I intend to become one, and I have followed a conventional path of having a job for most of my life.

However, if your interest lies not in where the puck is, but in where it's going, then consider becoming a creator—or at least give it a shot.

Yes, be careful and know that every game is a game of probabilities, with sometimes equal footing to success and failure. But treading carefully yet treading with awareness and confidence is where the stars of the Creator Economy will continue being born, and bloom.

In this chapter, we will understand the relationship a creator has with other three functioning elements of the Creator Economy.

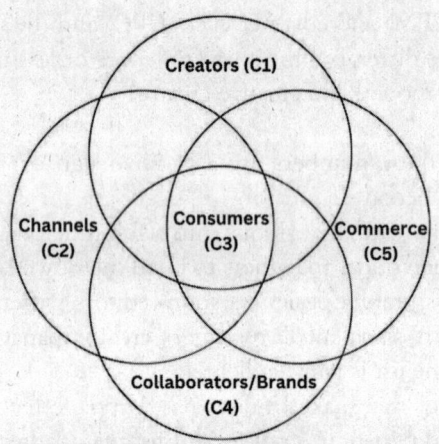

The 5Cs of the Creator Economy

4a: C1 and C4 (Creators and Brands)
4b: C1 and C2 (Creators and Channels)
4c: C1 and C5 (Creators and Commerce)
Let us dissect these in detail.

Chapter 4(a)

C1 <> C4: Creators and Collaborators (Brands)

The two most essential elements of the Creator Economy (other than the consumer, of course), are creators and collaborators (or brands).

If the Creator Economy has been a boon for creators, it has made a fortune for brands as well.

Creators: Because the economy thrives on the content they create.

Collaborators: Because more than 70 per cent of the revenue of creators comes from brand collaborations.

Both creators and collaborators have thus been functioning basis a customer-first strategy.

A customer-first strategy is a cultural method that puts the customer at the centre of everything that a business does.

For a creator, it means sharing authentic conversations through their content, so they build that trust with the customer.

For a brand, it means putting the creator first and putting revenue second.[3]

This virtuous cycle of brands working for creators working for an audience working for brands is what will only drive the

Creator Economy forward, one meaningful conversation and content piece at a time.

But before that, let us go to the time when brands and creators started working together.

In the years following the rise of social media platforms such as Facebook, Instagram, YouTube, etc., brands understood that the attention of the audience was on their devices, and hence expanded their advertising efforts to digital, from being previously restricted only to television, billboards and paper media. It was a natural extension because ads boom where attention blossoms. The Attention of most, if not all of their target audience as of now, is on their devices.

As per a 2024 report by GroupM, digital pure-play advertising was expected to account for account for 70.6 per cent ($699 billion) of total ad revenue of $989.8 billion in 2024.[4]

Here is how the brand spends on advertising in digital media is expected to rise:

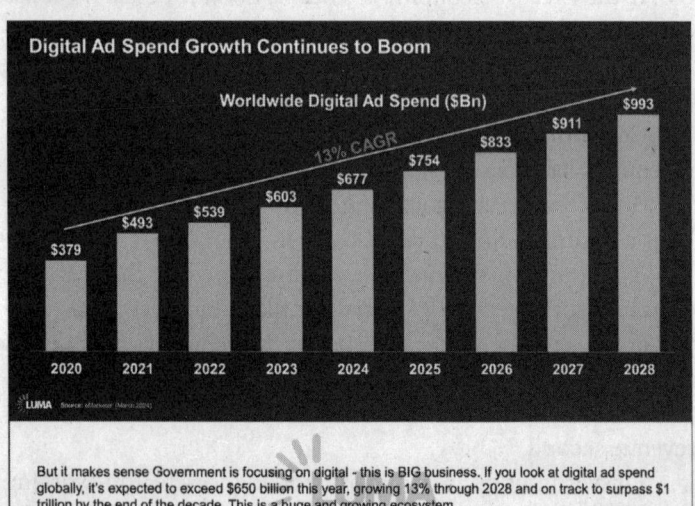

However, ad spends by brands on digital media had two problems:

1. Every social media platform favoured organic, user-generated content over advertised content. Thus, the leverage of digital ads had very little power since the very start.

2. As the users of every social media platform grew and started taking data and privacy more seriously, there were even greater barriers for brands to attract the eyeballs of the audience. For example, the 'Accept All Cookies' option that you get when you go to any website is basically text files with small pieces of data used to identify your computer and track your behaviour across websites. However, browsers like Google Chrome, Safari and Firefox are already on the way to ban cookies.

The user attention on the social media platforms only grew, nonetheless.

Creators also have the power to leverage brand shout-outs in their content, such as newsletters, podcasts, videos, where the creator actively mentions the brand and the brand pays to the creator directly, which could be a function of the number of click through actions (CTAs), views or a fixed amount based on the number of followers/subscribers the creator has.

As a result, brands have wisely begun shifting their focus to influencer marketing—working with content creators to promote products, increase awareness, or drive traffic to online stores—ensuring it all feels native to the consumer.

Why do brands need to collaborate with creators and influencers?

We will study the intricacy of how the Creator Economy aids brands in Chapter 4. For now, it is important to dissect why brands collaborate with creators and influencers, and how brand collaborations bring out the best for everyone: Creators, Collaborators (Brands) and most importantly: Consumers.

Let us analyse the three aspects of this reason for the existence of brands:

1. **To communicate their value on products/services:** In this, influencers can help brands by driving conversions. Along with that, brands can also leverage the power of television to draw brand awareness. While it is not possible to track the number of conversions, television is still a cheaper medium for brand awareness, especially in the emerging markets, because of infrastructural and internet bandwidth not being easily accessible in rural areas.

   In fact, India, the second-largest television household market in the world after China, has grown by a 1.1 per cent Compounded Annual Growth Rate from 2020 to 2023, reaching 217 million households. Not only that, while 65 per cent of Indian internet users watch ad-supported video content, nearly 75 per cent of Indian internet users still watch one or more pay TV services. With connected TVs expected to reach more than forty-five million households by the end of 2024, it is a fertile ground for brands to communicate their value on products and services.[5]

2. **By showcasing their value to their potential customers:** To showcase the value of their brand to potential customers, they need a bridge to connect with them. Collaborating with creators who have potential customers of those brands helps them with exactly that. For instance, I was consulting at a marketing agency start-up that had recently pivoted to creating podcasts as a strategy to attract more B2B clientele. During my discussions with them, it was pretty clear that they were

spending more time curating podcasts than actually building their product. Podcasting wasn't their core strength. They were not creators, and as a start-up the opportunity cost for them was too high. Yet, they felt this was an important marketing tactic.

What we did, instead, was this: I advised them to find early-mid stage podcasters in their field of work and partner with them by sponsoring a few episodes, thus ensuring the creator gives their business a callout. Or the start-up founder could even be a guest at a few podcasts by paying for the gig. This would ensure that:

The start-up was focused on building their product.

They did not have to reinvent the wheel (and build podcast audiences from scratch).

They might even be able to work out a long-term deal with one of the creators and optimize their spending (see next point below).

3. **Making profit in the process:** When a business makes profits, it can give back to the virtuous cycle of building more value and showcasing it to their potential customers, thus helping everyone in the cycle. Also, collaborating with creators and influencers gives a return on investment of $4.87 on every $1 spent[6] to the brand, which makes it cheaper for them, as compared to other campaigns.

As an outcome of all of this, the creator wins because they get paid to create content for their consumers; the consumers win because they are being shown a product from someone they trust; and the brands win because they are making higher return on investments than other sources of online ads.

Everyone wins when they understand how they do it.

That is why the Creator Economy is the biggest part of the overall digital marketing pie.

Thus, if we define a way, a roadmap, a structure for creators (even nano or micro creators) to work with brands (whether new brands or established brands), the Creator Economy will thrive in unlimited ways beyond what we can see currently.

Let us look at it through the lens of a 2*2 matrix, consisting of brands (or collaborators) on the x-axis, and creators on the y-axis.

The positive axis (top and right) stands for 'big' brands and creators; and the negative axis (bottom and left) stands for 'small' brands and creators.

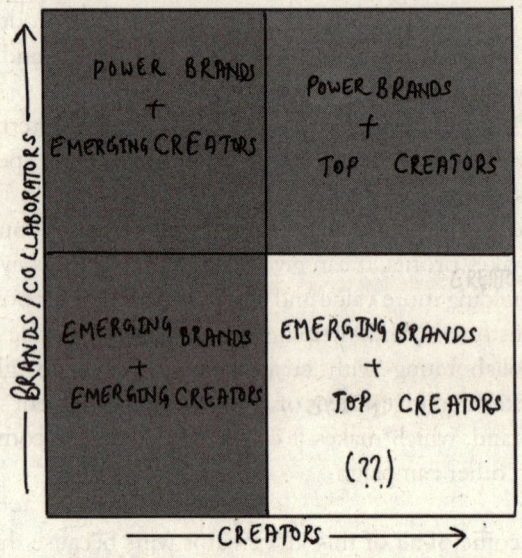

Four combinations emerge from this:
Power (big) brands work with top creators
Emerging brands work with top creators
Power brands work with emerging (nano and micro) creators
Emerging brands work with emerging creators

Of these, the first combination is the most obvious, and it's one many of us encounter in the Creator Economy:

Power Brands Working with Top Creators

An example is when MrBeast, the biggest creator on the planet, partnered with Samsung (one of the biggest collaborators/brands in the world) in September 2023, making the Samsung Galaxy smartphone series the official vlogging camera of Mr Beast.

Khaby Lame, mentioned earlier, partnered with one of the largest German clothing brands, Hugo Boss.

Prajakta Koli (previously MostlySane) endorses Gillette Venus as a part of a long-term partnership and is a classic example of an international brand working with a national mega creator to establish the presence of a relatively newer product line (hair removal for women) by a company that is better known for men's shaving products.

Collaborations like these are loud and luminous. They almost lay the path for brands and creators following their path globally.

Emerging Brands Working with Top Creators

The second quadrant of the 2*2 matrix, which is the bottom right side, is almost an impossible choice to begin with, because when you are a small brand, unless you get lucky and get a shout-out from a big creator, it is almost not a wise business decision to (maybe get into debt trap/burn all your investor money/business cash) spend exponentially on working with top creators.

There is a way, though.

Emerging brands are sometimes able to attract mega creators to be their ambassadors by way of equity (making the creator an investor in the company) or by sharing their profits.

Roger Federer is a classic example. When his partnership with Nike ended in 2018, that was also the time he wanted to help a Swiss brand create something cool. (For the uninitiated, Roger Federer is from Switzerland.) To quote the man himself, 'Let's do something different than just a classic ambassador collaboration or partnership. Let's make it more meaningful.'[7]

Thus began his partnership with the Swiss shoe brand, On.

But wait, didn't Federer partner with Uniqlo post his partnership ending with Nike?

He did. However, since Uniqlo was not into shoes, it basically gave Federer a blank canvas to explore shoe brands that he could partner with.

Enter On.

With what started as an off-court and an on-court shoe, the brand, today, has around ten on-court and off-court shoes in Federer's name, and hopefully more will join the kitty.

It is claimed that owning 3 per cent of the brand has made him richer than ever.

Another cool example that comes to mind is the Bollywood actor and global icon Deepika Padukone. Padukone, who has also been a presenter at the Academy Awards and jury at the Cannes Film Festival apart from her stellar record in the Bollywood film industry, has invested in brands like Mokobara and BLU Smart Taxi, among others.

Established in 2020, Mokobara is an internet-first brand that has come to fame for its creation of 'practically-fashionable' modern suitcases, luggage, duffels, backpacks and bags.

BLU-Smart is India's first zero-emission ride-hailing application, working towards creating a more sustainable future for upcoming generations. Established in 2019, it is currently leading in the all-electric ride hailing mobile services in India.

The holy grail, beyond equity and profit sharing with brands, is to work with small creators, grow into a prominent brand over time, and eventually rise to the top-right corner of the matrix.

A great very recent example that comes to my mind is Manu Bhaker, an Olympic shooter from India who secured two bronze medals in the 2024 Paris Olympics.

Unsurprisingly, Bhaker's success at the Olympics (for context, she is India's only Olympic double medallist) has seen her brand value soar five to six times, with her brand deals jumping from a few tens of thousands of dollars to hundreds of thousands, as over 50 brands now compete for her endorsements. What this means is, if an emerging brand had recognized her potential before she went for the Olympics and had signed a year-long deal, they would still be the member of an elite club with her, at her former, lower prices. Which is why the possibilities for emerging brands are endless; some of which occur by being at the right place at the right time.

Power Brands Working with Emerging Creators

Think of the marketing team of Apple sitting in their Cupertino headquarters, doing their usual work. Or think of the marketing team of Louis Vuitton in Paris, working with the original elite showstoppers, like they usually do.

Now think of your favourite nano or micro creator on social media who could be a perfect fit to market an iPhone or a Louis Vuitton bag.

And now, the million-dollar question: What is the possibility that these power brands are even aware of the existence of these small creators?

Close to zero. Nada. Zilch.

Which is where the biggest problem (as also the biggest opportunity!) stems in—a possible collaboration between power brands, nano and micro creators.

There are two facets to this situation: on the one hand, there are simply too many nano and micro creators so it is a mammoth task for the brands to identify the right creators to work with. Even if they do, they are still highly likely to miss out on a lot of creators, because there are so many across the globe.

On the other hand, it is an internal battle for nano and micro creators as well, to allow themselves to pitch their creativity to the power brands, because they do not have 'millions of followers'. Especially since the most visible collaborations of power brands are with mega influencers.

This is a classic problem where neither party makes the first move. A deadlock.

Which eventually becomes a classic example of neither party reaping the first mover advantage.

Here's some data from brands that will blow your mind:[8]

- Two in three brands are expanding their creator programmes in 2024.
- Of these, 43 per cent of brands would prefer long term partnerships with creators who prioritize prompt, professional communication.
- However, 81 per cent of brands claim to have less than five creators approaching them in a week. That's less than a creator per day.

All of this makes one thing clear:

There is potential. For brands to take in more creators. For creators to build more on their outreach and pitching. And for both of them together to make the Creator Economy more relatable and real to their mutual audiences/consumers.

Now that we know the theory, here comes the practical question:

How Is It Possible for Emerging Creators to Work With Power Brands?

I'd say this isn't done a lot.

But the brands that have taken this unconventional route, have done it unconventionally.

It might be helpful to note here that most businesses aim to maintain constant touchpoints with their consumers.

There are peak moments, such as a new product or feature launches where brands want to be top-of-mind to their consumers. And then there are plateau periods, where brands just aim to remain relevant and remembered.

Brands usually choose to engage with top creators for the peaks and with smaller creators for the plateaus.

For example, Audible collaborated on a campaign with photographer Jesse Driftwood, who had less than 1,00,000 followers on Instagram.

Rather than a sales pitch to promote Audible, Jesse shared his personal perspective on how using Audible helped him stay productive. The post received over 10,000 likes and 300 comments, with a 30 per cent engagement rate.

Or take the example of Forever 21, which encourages users to post pictures of their favourite outfits on their social media feed with the hashtag #F21xMe. In exchange for sharing content featuring Forever21 outfits, the engagement campaign pays influencers a flat fee with an apparel budget.

As we speak of big brands giving affiliate commissions, the global brand Nike also runs an affiliate programme in the US. It allows approved websites to earn commissions by promoting Nike products. It is a source for content creators, publishers and bloggers to monetize their traffic.

However, why would a big brand think of engaging a small creator if they can get the reach and revenue through top creators?

Here is why:

1. Emerging creators have a niche (and loyal) following. Their followers almost worship and know what their creator does.
2. This would especially be helpful in the plateau periods where the brand is looking to get closer to its consumer

through a more localized approach and/or create more brand awareness.

3. It is cost effective to work with small creators. Their prices haven't gone through the roof. Not yet.

4. Along with this, brands can also leverage special occasions where people are more likely to shop, such as Christmas and Black Friday, and extend their spray and pray experiments to attend to customer psychology that is attuned to shopping during this time.

5. Brands have more control over the narrative without having to lose their core identity or wanting the creator to lose their own.

6. If the approach works for the brand at the start and the creator is consistent in their content, the brand can also leverage that and engage the creator in a long-term partnership. This means that when they become macro or even mega, the brands would still be reaping the prices they paid when the creator was smaller.

However, in what cases is it still valuable for power brands to work with top creators? Here are some of those cases (of course, the list cannot be exhaustive for obvious reasons):

- During the peak periods, when the brand wants to get more sales.

  More eyeballs = more sales.

  More followers = more eyeballs.

  Macro/mega creator = more eyeballs.

- When a brand wants to establish trust and dependability. For example, Corporate Natalie, who has one million followers on Instagram and 7,00,000 on TikTok, is a mega and a macro creator. She works with Dell in more ways than one, such as collaborating for a video, addressing their interns and several other ad-hoc commitments for which they have newer contracts signed with her.

- When the brand is looking to build a long-term relationship. Roger Federer was Nike's brand ambassador for twenty-four years, before signing a $300 million, ten-year-year contract with Uniqlo in 2018, a Japanese clothing chain.
- A luxury or a niche product.
- Not a proven tactic, though it pays well sometimes when dealing with a sensitive brand topic. For example, in 2020, when Mint Mobile experienced network outages, Ryan Reynolds, the owner of the company and an actor known for his sharp wit, took to social media to acknowledge the issue in a self-deprecating and humorous way. This approach helped maintain a positive brand image and avoid a more serious PR disaster.

As a matter of fact, the top 20 per cent of the brands that invest in influencer marketing make more money and attract greater attention than the other 80 per cent of the brands in all stages of influencer marketing. These 20 per cent brands, also called as influencer marketing leaders, show:[9]

- 9.1x greater improvement in impressions (impressions = number of times the 'ad' or content piece was shown to audience)
- 8.2x greater improvement in engagement (engagement = number of likes/comments/shares of the content, i.e., any sort of reaction from the audience)
- 11.7x greater improvement in conversion rates (conversion rate = number of times the audience went ahead and bought because of influencer marketing)
- Happier, more loyal customers—with a 40 per cent higher profit margin, 38 per cent greater customer retention, 23 per cent more positive brand sentiment, and 16 per cent higher customer satisfaction compared to the remaining 80 per cent of brands.

This is not just plain vanilla numbers for a set of influencer marketing campaigns for the brands, influencer marketing has also driven 6.2x greater year-on-year improvement in annual revenue, and for every dollar these brands spend on influencer marketing, they make $4.70.

Key Areas	Influencer marketing leaders (top 20% brands)	Other brands (remaining 80%)	Overall difference
Average Customer Margin	51%	11.60%	4.8x
Customer Satisfaction	25.20%	8.40%	3x
Customer Retention	48.50%	9.80%	4.9x
Brand Sentiment	30.70%	7.20%	4.3x

Thus, it just makes sense for even emerging brands to dip their toes into working with emerging creators.

A return of $4.70 on every dollar spent on influencer marketing. That's an insane average.

It only makes sense for emerging brands to join the party.

The best part is that working with nano or micro creators won't cause the emerging brands to break their bank. Which, let's be honest, is an important metric when you are a small brand.

Also, I believe influencer marketing is a level field for brands of all sizes. Something that gets distorted with expensive, unpredictable and sometimes unmeasured traditional advertising mediums.

It is also prudent for emerging brands and emerging creators to look for alternate currencies of partnership beyond the cash.

Other than a flat cash fee, a small brand could pay the partner:

- A smaller flat fee + performance-based incentive based on pre-agreed performance metrics.

- Performance-based incentive based only on pre-agreed performance metrics.
- Affiliate commission where the creator makes a fixed percentage of the sale value.
- Gift or reward in kind (think barter)—such as a sponsored trip or beauty products.
- Discounts, in the form of store credits, discount vouchers, early product access, launch previews, etc.
- Stock options (wow!)

While we are discussing emerging brands, it is worth calling out an initiative known as Open Network for Digital Commerce (ONDC).

ONDC is an initiative by the Government of India, to transform the digital commerce ecosystem. Specifically for Small and Medium Enterprises (SMEs).

Set up in 2021, ONDC creates a fair and open digital commerce network to empower Indian SMEs.

They have partnered with a few e-commerce platforms that list the products of emerging brands, and buyers can shop their products (depending on the category) from these partner apps or websites.

These emerging brands (or SMEs) are thus able to reach a broader customer base. They also get healthy competition instead of having no chance against monopolistic markets. It also comes with the advantage of lower operating costs (of maintaining separate apps, marketing, distribution, etc.), thus reducing costs to the sellers as well as the buyers.

In a densely populated country like India, only 15,000 businesses have enabled e-commerce out of twelve million or so sellers. It is not even 0.2 per cent of the total.

The quick commerce platforms that deliver almost everything from vegetables to PlayStation and everything in between are mostly serving a few pin codes in Tier 1 cities.

Tier 2 cities, Tier 3 cities and rural areas are still out of that coverage. Partly because of the lower income bracket (and thus lower cost of living) in these areas, and partly because the fast-paced life of Tier 1 cities (unfortunately) demands quicker delivery of almost everything.

In such a situation, ONDC comes with the benefits of digital commerce without bringing in the arduousness of high cost of operating as Q-commerce.

It almost makes working with (digital) creators a no-brainer for small businesses. Think Amazon, LTK or any other marketplace affiliate programme.

Which is where the right education and the right encouragement from the right enabler (ONDC) would be worth gold to small businesses.

...

The Binding Glue of the Creator and Brand Partnership

Now that we have solved for the bottom right and bottom left quadrants, it is time to think of the binding glue of this brand and creator partnership: Duration of collaborations.

The duration of collaboration is a mutually agreed decision between the creator and the collaborator (brand). Thus, we will explore it differently from each of their perspectives.

Creator:

When starting out, a creator would want to engage in multiple short-term collaborations, so they understand:

- What their audience likes and engages with
- What kind of brand collaboration blows up (if it does)
- What kind of brand collaborations are a total no-no
- What kind of collaborations they are best positioned to voice through their content

- Most importantly, what kind of collaborations they enjoy and the kind they don't enjoy at all

Over time, as the creator has gathered enough data (and more followers) through the above learnings, they may decide to get into long-term partnerships with brands, considering:

- The commercial benefit it accrues
- The benefit and trust it would generate with their audience

Collaborator/Brand:

A brand would want to engage in one-time or short-term partnerships when:

- They are driving brand awareness
- Big ticket noisy events (festive sales, end-of-season sales, Cyber Monday, Black Friday sales, etc.)
- They are experimenting with new creators and want to dip their toes into the water before diving into the pool fully.

However, in the following cases, a brand would want to work with long-term gigs, that too with fewer creators:

- Build a lasting relationship with their audience (Did you know the customer needs to see a product at least 7x, before they buy it?[10]
For example, Dell Computers noticed a laptop in some of Corporate Natalie's videos (the content creator), and reached out to her. They started working initially through an agency, but now she works with them directly—either through group texts, sending a draft of her video for feedback, going to represent Dell at

events, or even consulting their Gen Z interns. Almost like an employee.

Isn't the whole episode of partnership and how content can literally take you places quite epic? As a matter of fact, a decision-maker in a company who follows Natalie's videos would rather trust her more than a movie star promoting the same computer, because Natalie has established trust.

- Have new launches lined up and want to build awareness about the brand before the launch.
- Want to define themselves with the identity of a creator. For example, Uniqlo's ten-year partnership with Roger Federer, that started in 2018, will make the former world number one earn $30 million per year. This move made Federer forgo a 24-year partnership with Nike.

In a conference about his association with Uniqlo, Federer said: 'I stand for style on the court. I really wanted to make the best apparel, the best-looking apparel for a tennis player in recent years, obviously I want to redo that, create the coolest things with Uniqlo, [it] is something I'm very excited about. And I'm also going beyond that into lifewear.'

I can only imagine the impact a humble, yet super-achieving athlete's words would have on aspiring athletes and the brand itself.

Dealing with the Brand Money as a Creator

As a creator, it's crucial to understand how to leverage the brand's investment to your advantage.

Sometimes, brands insist on controlling the narrative by deciding how much of the callout the creator would make, the language they would speak and the duration of the callout (if it is a video).

If it goes with the creator's narrative, the creator should go about doing it. However, if the creator speaks a different creative language, it is best that the creator bends the brand narrative into what they do and speak.

If the creator just goes about saying what the brand says without truly believing in it, it breaks their audience's trust. The audience is now smart enough to know 'this creator got paid hence they changed their usual dynamic to accommodate the brand'.

Not just that content piece—a loyal fan base will also look at you as someone who left their authenticity for money.

While I say that, I do not undermine the importance of brand deals.

A brand looks for influencers who get the right eyeballs for their products. As an influencer, engaging in brand deals is as pious as a movie star signing movie deals. You just have to pick the one that serves your audience, not take them away.

Conclusion:

As you can see, the collaborator and creator partnerships are a greenfield opportunity: Infinite, ever expanding and you can go in the direction that works for you at the moment, and pivot when you need to.

There is something for everyone in the Creator Economy.

Key takeaways:

- Along with the creators, the Creator Economy has created a fortune for brands as well.
- Brand deals account for 70 per cent of the creators' main source of revenue
- Brands exist for three reasons: 1. To communicate their value to existing customers. 2. To showcase their value to potential customers. 3. To make profit in the process.

- When they tick all three boxes right, brand collaborations with creators create magic for the consumers. And of course, themselves.
- Brands work with creators. Creators work for consumers. Consumers drive the brands' business. It's a virtuous cycle where the brands come to the front.
- With the rise of social media platforms, brands started investing heavily in their ads as well on these platforms.
- However, social media platforms run on algorithms. Algorithms tend to prioritize organic content over ads in user feeds. At the same time, ads that show up on feeds aren't very comfortable for the users since they fear their privacy being compromised. With all of this, the middle path was for brands to collaborate with creators who create an audience for the brand's. It helps them reach out to the right audience without dealing with the negative consequences of paid ads, also called influencer marketing.
- Creators and brands have leverage over the influence they exert, depending on their size (big or small). Based on that, four combinations emerge: Power brands and top creators; emerging brands and top creators; emerging brands and emerging creators; power brands and emerging creators.
- Brands earn a return of investment (ROI) of $4.70 on every $1 spent on influencer marketing.

Chapter 4(b)

C1 <> C3: Creators and Channels (Platforms)

When Instagram was raw in the 2012–2014 era, you won't believe how you used to grow as a creator back then.

No, not reels. (Reels was launched as a feature in 2020.)

Nope, not IGTV (Instagram TV) either. (For the noobs, IGTV was a long video feature of Instagram that enabled sharing of videos longer than 60 seconds. Launched in 2018, the feature is now embedded in reels itself.)

So, how did we grow on Instagram?

By using hashtags.

Yes, you read that right.

Underneath the caption of every picture or a video that was posted on Instagram, the creator would also add fifteen to twenty hashtags that would give them a wider reach to their relevant audience.

Isn't it crazy how far we have come? Also, isn't it scary how far we have come?

Scary, because the creators that were dependent on hashtags for their growth (and saw exponential growth because of hashtags) were now wondering for months and years about where their reach had gone.

The creators who had been putting in their work for years had nowhere to go. This is the magic as well as the misfortune of algorithms. They make the invisible visible and the visible redundant.

Algorithms are probably like smartphones. They make the resourceful feel powerful, while those with abundant resources become addicted.

Since we are talking about algorithms, we have to talk about Twitter (now X) and its acquisition by Elon Musk in the year 2022.

Up until 2022, Twitter was a prime space for creators to showcase their tweetstorms and share useful information.

As of 2024, it still has a lot of creators (and the most influential personalities) there, however, the number of creators complaining about the reach going down on the platform in the post-Musk hellscape is insane. It's yin and yang at its peak in the Creator Economy.

However, if someone like Elon Musk buys a company for $44 billion, there must be (and probably is) something that is still working about the company.

Here are a few things that happened after Elon Musk took over the company:

Creators on X now get paid every quarter for crossing a certain threshold of impressions. It is a good incentive for creators to continue creating, especially since content creation on Twitter was never monetized for creators before.

Anyone can get their account verified by paying a nominal subscription fee every month. I believe it is a good way for legit creators to establish their authenticity.

The size of a tweet, now renamed as 'post', has expanded from 280 to 4,000 characters. A much-needed upgrade.

The creator can also add their most important messages in the Highlights tab that is placed next to the Posts and Replies tabs on everyone's profile. Elon Musk has also claimed posts in Highlights to have more reach.

Likes are now private. This means, only I can see what I liked, and you can see what you liked. Neither of us can go onto each other's profiles and stalk each other about what we are liking. This privacy is also a baller move as it allows the creator to see what they like yet being private about not wanting to see their engagement.

I am still bullish about the platform and hope for Elon to turn it around. However, I am also a creature of rationality, data and user feedback.

Which is why we can also not ignore the humongous number of creators who have either lost their motivation to create on X because of the changed algorithm, or even when they sustained the motivation and kept up with the change, the algorithm still had only vanity to offer. Paul Graham, who is the founder of the start-up accelerator Y Combinator and one of the more consistent creators on X, also has a similar insight to offer for the platform:

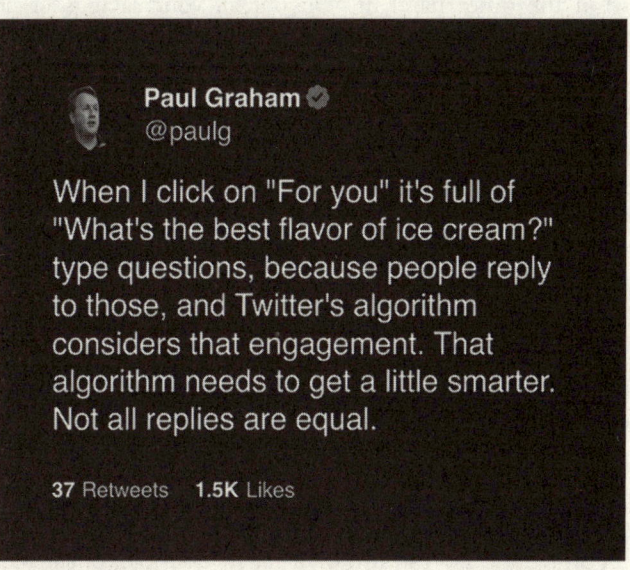

So, what's the way out?

Should we quit the Creator Economy altogether?

Running away is rarely the answer, ever.

The Creator Economy is also the attention economy. It is where everyone's attention is. So, as an alternative route, I would like to think that the Creator Economy is like an investment in equities or stocks.

Should we invest in stocks? Yes, we should.

Do we make money on stocks? Yes, most people do, considering they: 1. Pick their bets wisely. 3. Review their portfolio once in 6-12 months, not daily or on market gloom and doom days. 3. Stay invested for long.

Is it risky to invest in stocks? I bet it is.

So, if you put all your savings in stocks, you risk losing everything during a market downturn while you are casually sipping coconut water on a beach in the Maldives.

On the other hand, if you put all your savings in non-risky assets such as term deposits, you might not make enough returns to be able to afford a flight to Maldives, let alone sip coconut water there.

The answer is to carry the classic Warren Buffet advice of the stock market to the Creator Economy: *Don't put all your eggs in one basket*.

What I am trying to say is, it is wise for you as a creator brand to not depend on just one platform as your source of followers and income.

Every platform that is loved and has seen massive adoption has also seen a change in their algorithm. Be it Instagram, Facebook, X or LinkedIn. Or worse, if you were a creator on Vine, MySpace or TikTok from a remote village in India, not only did algorithms pose a challenge, but your content and social identity also faced an existential crisis.

Forgive me for the use of a harsh example, but it means slogging very hard to build a commercial property of yours that pays you well, only to wake up to an earthquake and see it go under the debris.

You don't want to put yourself in that position, right?

That is why it is a wiser (and a more strategic) option to hedge that risk.

Here is how it would help you:

You leverage the new audience of that platform and the total addressable market (TAM), which is equivalent to millions and billions of users. This means that a new platform that is booming and has attracted your attention as a creator also has a ready audience that allows the creator to thrive. It could range from a few million to billions of users. It's a ripe market waiting to be acquired.

You understand the flavour of each platform and how they cater differently to the same audience. A consumer might scroll through reels for entertainment during work hours, browse X for sharp opinions, wander around LinkedIn for job opportunities or industry updates, and turn to YouTube for how-to videos.

You get out of your comfort zone. You are a beginner again. You are learning. It is like opening new outlets by a food or hospitality chain—it is not only costing, it is also the location, customer mindset, customer preferences and dealing with consequent unexpected failures.

However, I understand if you are a part-time or a full-time creator, time is always scarce. You barely get time to be consistent on one platform initially, expanding on the other one is just doubling the efforts.

Impossible.

What if there is a way?

What if you don't have to make fresh content every time? What if you could use the same content of your dominant platform and use it to create dominance in other places?

How could you do that?

If you create reels on Instagram, start repurposing them on YouTube shorts as well.

If you create text content on X, take a screenshot of it and post it on LinkedIn with a few words about how the one-liner adds value to your work life (Note: LinkedIn is a work-specific platform). Alternatively, use that screenshot to create a reel on Instagram, add music from its vast gallery and give it the right look and feel.

If you run a newsletter, promote it on one of your social channels consistently. A newsletter is basically a deep dive into your unique insights. Whereas on social media, a creator usually shares who they are and what they do, in different ways and formats. Since your audience would love to know more about the work you do, you can link your newsletter at the end of some organic posts, and boom—you now have your own content distribution.

If you create long-form YouTube videos, you can create relevant, contextual snippets for different platforms, tailored to their unique purpose, and post them on Instagram, LinkedIn, Facebook or even X.

The possibilities are endless.

The audience often forgets what you did three months ago, three weeks ago, or even three days ago. Why not make the best use of that to re-share your journey?

Having a presence on multiple platforms can lead to more brand collaborations which will not only help you grow your presence but also grow your business.

Also, a brand or a collaborator will see your multi-channel presence as an indication that you take your brand seriously to be doing the hard work in more than one place..

PS: If you want to learn from someone who has actually dug their toes into the muddy waters, Gary Vaynerchuk, the OG content creator from Manhattan, owner of multiple businesses, and one of the most confident guys on the internet, came up with a content deck of how he creates more than sixty-four pieces of content in a week.

This might be helpful:

Is it difficult?

Well, good things worth doing are difficult.

However, you must remember one thing as a content creator:

If you can do the difficult task of being consistent with creating content on one platform as practice, the rest is just mimicking the same with 20 per cent effort and 100 per cent results.

Smart businesspeople, which every content creator is, figure out a way to make that investment.

Key takeaways:

- The platforms go through their own cycles of growth, where their algorithms are bound to change.
- Therefore, a wise creator, like a wise investor, would do what Warren Buffet suggested: Don't put all your eggs in one basket.
- A creator should strategically figure to repost the content of their existing platform to another platform, while making sure they align with the language and tonality of the new platform they are venturing into.
- If you can do the difficult task of being consistent with creating content on one platform as practice, the rest is just mimicking the same with 20 per cent effort and 100 per cent results.

Chapter 4(c)

C1 <> C5: Creators and Commerce

Brand partnerships are a goldmine.

For the creators. For the brands. For the customers.

This is especially true because 70 per cent of a creator's revenue comes from brand partnerships.

However, like a true investor, a creator would not put all their eggs in one basket.

When that basket is thriving, it feels too good to let go. When that basket is bearish, it feels foolish to not let go of your assumptions.

Therefore, if you've built leverage as a content creator, make the most of it to share the best of your learnings with your audience.

When we talk about making the most of sharing your learnings, let me share a painful example that every creator goes through:

...

When you are a creator, you wear different hats at the same time.

Ideation.

Planning your content.

Execution.

Analysing data.

Listening to customer feedback.

Putting all of that into the ideation process again.

Rinse and repeat.

Not to forget the 'pre-scheduling' work if you are a consistent creator and are going on a break.

If a creator wants to start their own small online store offering digital products or consultations, it is not only difficult, but also nearly impossible. It's not easy to have the time and the energy to set up a Shopify store, build it from scratch, integrate payment software, integrate their website, and put all of that together.

In my experience working with nano and micro creators, many find it overwhelming to the point where the entrepreneur-creator considers abandoning their idea of an online store to avoid the hassle.

It is all the more difficult for a creator to make this investment, especially if they have just started to make ends meet in the Creator Economy.

In this case, I stumbled onto Topmate at just the right time.

As a business, Topmate helps creators to:

- Put all their digital products (e-books, PDFs) together in one place (without having to create their own website)
- Offer 1:1 consultation (in any currency)
- Have monthly subscriptions
- Host webinars
- It is a free tool that only charges 7 per cent–10 per cent commission on your sales, based on the features you pick. The best part? You can withdraw your money anytime, in a single click.

Clearly one of the most robust platforms the Creator Economy has been blessed with.

This comes as an add-on to the last chapter where we spoke about the decline and death by algorithms.

As brands evolve and continue to bloom online, a resource like Topmate is like health insurance—when everything fails, it makes you feel rich.

...

The brands not only rely on algorithms to make ends meet, but also make ends blossom by now working (and creating more relationships with their customers and upselling to them often).

Other examples where you could do the same are:

Creating your courses:

Tony Robbins and Robin Sharma, who have been the OG leaders of the Creator Economy, have created their courses, and successfully scaled them before the Creator Economy grew to where it is today, and they continue to do so.

Gagan Biyani, the founder of Maven and former co-founder of Udemy, both course platforms, has a unique take on this:

When we started Udemy every investor we talked to asked us: 'Why wouldn't Google or YouTube just do this?'

This is the answer. You can't learn shit with 10-minute viral videos.

You gotta go deep, spend dedicated time. Your life will change as a result.

Courses give you in-depth knowledge of the creator's mind, which goes wide and further than their content, thus giving the consumer an added knowledge of things they want and a chance to monetize their knowledge.

The platform Kajabi, that we spoke of in Chapter 3, has made it all the easier by combining all elements of a creator's world into one. The best part is, you don't have to pick from one. Maven (which is a course hosting platform) built by Wes Kao, who also built Seth Godin's AltMBA, is another excellent platform.

I will not be surprised if more platforms come to the scene by virtue of more creators creating their own courses.

Newsletters:

A creator could drive their audience to their newsletter, which gives them the following advantage:

Getting access to their emails, where, along with sharing their specialized knowledge, the creator could also add links to their services/products.

Newsletter platforms such as Convertkit (now Kit) have also launched its Creator Network where creators can recommend other creators and be recommended by other creators while the subscriber is signing up.[11] When one wins, the other also wins. And vice versa.

Substack, which is another newsletter platform, allows the creator to create a paid newsletter, where the subscribers will pay a monthly subscription fee, to have access to the specialized knowledge of the creator.

A niche newsletter with a decent audience of over 5000 would also be able to attract brand sponsorships worth hundreds of dollars. These are typically products from brands that have the same audience as you and want to leverage your audience to drive conversions or brand awareness.

Creating Your Own Merchandise/Product:

A joy amongst the Gen Z audience, specifically for Instagram creators. Mugs, t-shirts, journals go as creative as you can, and dedicated fans will love to be affiliated. Phone cases by The Slow Mo Guys, or t-shirts by The Try Guys and Ashish Chanchlani are all examples of fan love from the creator to the audience in the currency of merchandise.

Or get as cool, crazy and creative as MrBeast and launch a product no one expected you to: a dark chocolate chain. I dare not miss out the Kylie Cosmetics or Cameron Dallas clothing line or Rare Beauty by Selena Gomez. These are the creators' ways of reaching the audience's home. And heart.

Exclusive Content on Patreon:

Patreon is a platform for podcasters, video creators, musicians, artists or game developers to create exclusive content for their fans, which they can direct from their presence on other social media platforms.

...

I, by no means, am diluting the importance of the Creator Economy, the one that thrives on the platforms. I would be the last person to do it.

However, a wise business makes use of the Creator Economy instead of making the Creator Economy make use of them. You create your economy from the Creator Economy.

Thus, creating commerce outside of channels is an absolute extension of the success of thriving on the Creator Economy.

It all boils down to the first principles of business:

Keep looking around. What you think is an opportunity might become a threat. Alternatively, what you currently identify as a fluke might be the fulcrum.

Be friends with the Creator Economy, but don't be friends only with the platform (channel), become friends with the commerce apps as well. And the Creator Economy will never stop giving to you.

Key takeaways:

- Brand sponsorships account for nearly 70 per cent of a creator's business revenue. However, if a creator only focuses on that, they are hedging too much on the side of a probable negative, and not leveraging the commerce they could build out of their existing audience.
- Some ways for creators to leverage this are: 1:1 consultations, hosting webinars, selling digital products, creating courses, building a newsletter following and selling sponsorships, creating merchandise, creating products, and creating exclusive content. If you were to be a little creative, the list is literally endless.

Chapter 4(d)

The Power of Plenty or the Problem of Plenty?

Here is a fun fact most people would have forgotten: The first iPhone used to come with these apps—Phone, Contacts, Messages, Photos, Stocks, Weather, Clock, Calculator, Calendar, Notes and Settings.

That's it.

As you can see, there was no swipe function to the next screen. Fun fact: There wasn't any app store in the first place.

Imagine living in a world where you had no WhatsApp on your smartphone.

Today, when you get a new smartphone, almost every app that matters is pre-installed. Facebook, Instagram, Snapchat, LinkedIn, Email, WhatsApp, Facebook Messenger, Netflix and Amazon Prime video.

To talk in terms of Creator Economy, someone becoming a creator now does not even have to take the pains of installing the app. They can get on board the minute they decide to.

Not only the big players.

The creator universe is expanding infinitely in smaller, more emerging markets. Along with the bigger players, smaller players like Likee in Indonesia, Josh in India and other similar apps are gaining traction and building forward momentum.

There is power of plenty as every platform has a category of its users that a new creator can cater to.

However, there is a problem of plenty—so many apps and communication channels, such as Instagram DMs, LinkedIn DMs, emails, and WhatsApp. We're not making the best of any platform, neither as creators, consumers, nor as brands or marketers

It's like a buffet dinner. Looks pleasing when you are invited to one, ravishing when you look at the dishes, delicious when you devour the multiple food items. But do it daily, and your health, digestion, abs and muscles are doomed, no matter how fit and healthy you used to be before.

Having more platforms does exactly that. A creator may think it would mean expanding frontiers and gaining new and wider audiences, but it also means diminished focus and declining quality.

As a consumer, we might want to scroll reels to be entertained, be on YouTube to see reaction videos, Twitch to watch or stream live events, have some creative humour watching bite-sized videos on (once existing) Vine, get ideas for decorating our interiors and cakes and wardrobe and what not on Pinterest, be a part of the casual communication lifestyle through streaks on Snapchat, and be on LinkedIn to be informed of what is up and new in the corporate ecosystem, but it also means giving in to a never-ending urge for dopamine and feeding it to become more anxious, less worthy and never really keeping up with anything!

As a marketer, it is even worse because their job is basically to arrive at an intersection of mentally drained out creators and consumers, create something 'viral' every single day, and keep an eye out for social conversations where the brand could potentially tap into.

It is difficult to thrive at the best intersection of all.

There is power that comes with plenty, and there is power that goes away with plenty.

'With great power comes great responsibility,' as a *Spider-Man* comic once said.

We can take responsibility only when we are aware of how we can do it. Because when human beings are massively aware of their potential, they end up building an entire Creator Economy. So, guarding themselves against the use of it could be a cakewalk.

Key takeaways:

- Not only big apps with billions of users, but regional apps are also gaining traction amongst creators. Especially in the emerging markets.
- The audience (consumers) have multiple options to get their dopamine hit. After all, there is a plethora of content and creators.
- The condition is worse for marketers. Because they still have to figure out a way of creating 'viral and original' content while they struggle to hold an audience with less attention span than a goldfish.
- There is power in plenty. But when used too much, it becomes a poison, as goes the adage 'excess of everything is poison'.
- The right way is to do your own thing on social media, have some dopamine hit (maybe 30–60 minutes a day), and then, make it extinct from the rest of the day, for you to 'deserve' it the next day. And so on.

Chapter 4(e)

Mental Health for Creators

As a creator, life is no different from being an entrepreneur.

You start with an idea.

You start with a risk.

You put out your first minimum viable product into the market.

You keep shipping.

You listen to customer feedback.

You iterate.

Rinse and repeat.

After months and years of hard work, self-doubt and watching other creators in your niche thrive, you are finally able to make it in the Creator Economy.

However, the Creator Economy is also a fast-moving world.

What was thriving yesterday is no longer relevant today.

One fine day, the algorithm changes.

Other days, a different platform becomes more relevant.

The next week, your USP, the thing that made you thrive as a creator, is no longer working on the platform for anyone.

Or something beyond your control—the platform is acquired or banned in your country.

If all is good, the tastes of audiences evolve over time.

On top of all that, you are being vulnerable and putting yourself out there every day.

Being on the edge and innovating consistently.

Learning from (and competing with) other creators and constantly sharpening your game.

Thus, being a creator is as much a job of pressure as running a start-up. Sometimes even more, because you are shipping content every day, sometimes multiple times a day.

So, how do you deal with it?

What do I have to offer you beyond a Google search that you could see to take care of your mental health?

Here are some learnings I have derived from working with creators on the ground:

1. Set boundaries for privacy

For a Certain number of your waking hours, don't use your devices. Even if your work runs and thrives on devices, it is not impossible for anyone to get off their devices for some time.

It will help you take care of your mind which is constantly bombarded with 'data' while using digital devices, give it its much-needed space, and most importantly, that boundary is where you will have better ideas for execution, when you get back.

2. Define a schedule of your work

Some creators like to divide their days into chunks: Meetings in certain parts of the day only. Creative work in other parts. Other creators divide their weeks into chunks: Available for meetings the whole day on certain days. Creative work the whole day on other days.

Being a creator (often) gives you the freedom to define your own schedule. Using that privilege helps everyone you work with more than it helps you. Because they understand you are committed to your work.

3. Invest in real life relationships

Yes, bonding with other creators is crucial.

Vlogging with them or creating a dance reel or merely just hanging around with someone who goes through similar pains and gains as a creator is something every creator must do.

However, a very important part of having a sane life as a creator is having relationships outside of your Creator Economy ecosystem.

People who understand absolutely nothing about your job.

People who want to hang around with you, the person; not for what you have done.

People who are unlikely to read this book.

These relationships ground you, help you stay connected to your roots, and consistently remind you that you as a person are much more than your achievements and content.

The content people outside of the content world are probably the OG content of a more meaningful life.

4. Create small, munchable goals

This reminds me of a quote from another creator, author and speaker, Robin Sharma:

Dream big. Start small. Act now.

Setting the loftiest goals is not only unusual, but also right. How will you land those goals if you don't set them?

However, if I plan to run a marathon but never get to touch the treadmill in the gym, how will I ever get there?

So, my friend, start small. If you have 10,000 followers, aim to get to the next 10,000 in 75 per cent of the time. The next 10,000 takes 60 per cent of the time.

If you have got one brand collaboration in a month, try getting two next month, not twelve.

Over time, as you gain confidence, consistency and course correction, you can (and must) always set bigger goals. My experience in sports also says that the player with the best results is the player that worked minimally on their goals, not monumentally.

5. 'You are NOT your social media account'

Now, this is hard for some people to believe, considering they put out everything on their social media.

What I am trying to say is your social media makes your business, and you should treat it with the emotions of a business.

You run a business. Your Business runs on putting yourself out there (by creating content about your life, often).

You are not a business. The business will not run on burning yourself out.

This distinction is very important to make because before your community and followers and brands and platforms, the biggest relationship you have is with yourself.

When you draw that boundary, you run it like a businessperson: Strategic. Committed. Dedicated. Disciplined. But not attached.

It often helps you make rational decisions.

6. The power of team

Let's be practical: you won't have a team as big as MrBeast or Joe Rogan, especially at the micro, nano or even macro stage. However, a small team of interns can help delegate work that:

- You don't fully enjoy doing
- But is important for your business
- You want to get done

Another way to make this happen is to employ people in a roster. To each their own, however, it might be worthwhile to consider this idea.

It not only saves your time (which is your most important resource), you all also become each other's support system when one person feels low, sounding boards when needed, and you celebrate with each other when you succeed.

7. You don't have to do it alone

Even with a team, let's face the facts: no one can understand your brand as much as you do, being the face and owner as a creator.

For example, Brent Rivera: his sister Lexi, their friends Andrew, Ben, Pierson, Jamie and many others are YouTubers with millions of followers and come under the umbrella digital studio Amp World (which was started by Brent Rivera). These YouTubers not only appear consistently in each other's videos, they are also best friends with each other. Amp World also has a dedicated YouTube and Instagram channel, and the power of co-creation is clearly visible in those fun videos.

Now, even if one of them is going through mental health issues, they still have a community of friends who might have gone through the same stuff or are just there to support.

MrBeast started on YouTube by simply discussing the platform with his buddies—over the years.

The power of communities is very helpful, especially for a creator, because only creators understand what other creators go through.

8. Lastly, get help if needed

There used to be a time when seeking help on mental health issues was taboo. Fortunately, we are long past a society that used to scoff when we told them we were seeking therapy.

In the world (and more so the Creator Economy world) we live in, seeking therapy is not a curative measure. It is almost a preventive measure.

It keeps you in perspective, helps you vent what is clogging your mind, and lets you see the movie of your life as a creator and create the movie you want to be living in.

After all, you are a creator, right?

Some apps that also do a great job of having you take care of your mental health are Calm and Headspace. Even YouTube has some great meditations to lead the way.

However, sometimes the most important effort you can make is to take even just one minute to meditate, especially if you can't manage ten, thirty, or sixty. It's the small, seemingly insignificant steps that create significance over time.

...

An estimated 26 per cent of American adults (1 in 4 people) go through mental health issues.[12] That is a whopping 12 per cent more than adults suffering from diabetes in the US (14.7 per cent).[13] The numbers are far higher in developing countries where mental health wellness is still not well recorded.

To put this in perspective, more people are suffering from mental illnesses than diabetes, the biggest lifestyle disease of all time. This is only the reported number, sometimes people are not aware either, that they are going through mental health issues.

I share this stat not to scare you, rather to reassure you, that if you are going through as a creator, a wiser idea will be to not look at it as a part of your life as a creator and take the steps you know that will make your mental health better. Remember, even a physically fit person could go through an injury or fall sick.

After all, the world needs creators who bring their best into everything they create. This is only possible when you let go of everything that holds your mind back, allowing it to be free to create at its best.

Key takeaways:

- Being constantly in the public eye is no mean feat. A lot of 'celebrities' have experienced depression, even before the exponential growth of the Creator Economy suffered.

- As a creator, when you have a camera on yourself, you are constantly in the public eye; it sometimes puts pressure on you to behave in a certain way.
- Plus, being a creator is no less than running a start-up. It's sometimes more difficult.
- Thus, practical preventive and curative steps are wise for sound mental health as a creator.
- Remember, you're here to play the long game. Like a marathon runner who wouldn't sprint their first or even fifteenth mile, you need to be progressive in your content creation journey.

Chapter 5

The Future of the Creator Economy

Through the pages of this book, we have spoken about a lot of my experiences.

Experiences that have shaped my understanding of the Creator Economy.

Experiences that I think would be useful to you to form yours.

Experiences that I didn't know would someday form a part of my first ever book!

However, in this chapter, I want to take a spin. Instead of experiences, I want to share an experiment.

An experiment of a peek into the future.

An imagined story, if you will.

Of course, we won't be speaking about flying cars (wish we get to see them one day). However, what we will be speaking about is how our Creator Economy would fly off to remarkable places and heights beyond our wildest imagination.

Let's imagine a day in our lives in 2035.

I wake up in the morning to my humanoid robot, playing my latest music preference.

It has already gauged from my movements in my sleep, the time I am about to wake up. Thus, it has kept my bedside tea ready, to be piping hot when I wake up. Exactly how I would want it.

As I wake up, the humanoid robot gets me my tea and displays the latest global news—which I can read, watch, or listen to. Of course, my humanoid is aware of my personal news preferences and serves it to me accordingly.

I blink my eyes for the articles I find interesting, and they are automatically bookmarked for my later reading.

As I move into my study, the virtual screens on my desk light up. Did I tell you that laptops are obsolete by now? (I still have one just for the memories, since you don't get them at the store any more).

Anyway, after working for a bit, mostly with my finger sensors and brain scans, I am now going for an in-person meeting. So, my humanoid shares the weather report and route for me, books an electric cab and suggests some lunch options based on my diet preferences and taste.

All I have to do is just show up.

During my commute, the humanoid shows me the exact notes of conversation with the person I am going to meet, after scanning them through my emails, WhatsApp and LinkedIn messages. It has also given me a cool personality reveal of the person I am going to meet, based on their online profiles.

The meeting goes well.

As I am on my way back, I look for entertainment and social media content on the screen in the cab itself. It turns out, all the content is curated for me based on my history.

It's not just organic content, but also AI-generated content with different 'hooks' and 'endings' tailored specifically for my experience, or the usual content that AI serves me based on my preferences. In other words, no one consumes the content that I do—and vice versa.

Also, did I tell you I can now check all my social media accounts on the same platform? It is all universally located in one place. It is the Fediverse.

Also, which app is Fediverse located on?

None. Because I consume it on my glasses, and Fediverse is omnipresent on the glasses, just like the operating systems of our smartphones.

Later, I come across a cool t-shirt a man is wearing, and I'm able to purchase it with just three blinks—not clicks.

I also purchased a similar virtual t-shirt for my digital twin who would be giving a talk tomorrow at VidCon in the US, since I won't be able to attend it in person. No worries at all, since I have already reviewed the notes, and my digital twin is prepared to speak on my behalf.

While we are talking about my digital twin, I also want to tell you about my avatar for all things gaming, which unlocks digital currency that I can redeem in the physical world. They are synonymous with cash, just like cryptocurrencies. Yes, my friend, if it was not clear already, you can use them for trading NFTs.

Except that this is a positive, progressive and tech-functional world, quite contrary to Ernest Cline's depiction of a dystopian futuristic world in *Ready Player One*.

Anyway, now I am back home on my living room couch, where the holograms of my favourite podcaster and their guest are waiting for me. It kicks off only when I snap my fingers. Fun fact: I can ask questions on the go and not only get answers, but the podcast also fine-tunes itself to my flow of questions. This is how I sign off for the day. And my humanoid, already aware of how my day went and how my past few weeks have been, knows exactly what to serve me tomorrow.

Good night, folks.

...

Scary? Exciting? Boring?

There could be many expressions. I'd say all of them are fair reactions.

There is a fact about the future. It is inevitably wildly different from our best guess.

The other fact is something that we all might be quietly ignoring, but ignorantly aware of: The internet experience of today is the least sophisticated it will ever be.

So, fasten your seatbelts, all you curious Creator Economy constituents. The future of the Creator Economy is going to be one hell of a ride. The past has already shown us how.

Chapter 5(a)

Evolutions That Led to Revolutions

As a creator, life is no different from being an entrepreneur.

You start with an idea.

Once every few decades, there's a revolution which changes earth's landscape. Forever.

Things were never the same after the vaccine for smallpox was invented. Or when scientific revelations by Copernicus, Galileo, Sir Isaac Newton and the like revolutionized our understanding of the world in the sixteenth century. Or the French Revolution started in the late eighteenth century and inspired movements for democracy and social reform in the entire world.

Similarly, things were never the same after the precursor to the Internet (ARPANET—Advanced Research Projects Agency Network) was developed in 1969 by the United States Department of Defense's Advanced Research Projects Agency (ARPA).

This led to the starting of a generation of internet many years later that was called Web 1.0. These were the starting days of the internet, where there was no 'communication' or 'social media' and websites were merely brochures or repositories of information.

As Web 1.0 reached its maturity and stagnation, it made way for Web 2.0 in the early 2000s, also known as the era of social media—where users could interact with each other, instead of just browsing static web pages. It was also the lever to put the Creator Economy into action, because of the ability to share content online and have participation from the audience.

Now, as the Web 2.0 has reached its peak, it has been slowly making way (maybe it has already made way) for Web 3.0, also known as the Semantic Web, where we are entering into a decentralized economy to create a more open and transparent internet ecosystem, where users have greater control over their digital assets.

All of the new revolutions have been built on the backbone of the revolutions behind them and have collectively contributed to the growth of our culture. including the Creator Economy.

What I mean to say is that the seeds of any revolution are sown in the events of the past that lead up to the tipping point.

Widespread communication through handwritten letters coupled with expensive phone calls triggered the internet, which was both cheaper and faster. Thus, it went on to become Web 1.0.

When the communication through emails or phone calls was taken care of, there came the need for another form of communication: Being socially connected with people you know. It eventually expanded to people you didn't know, thus leading to communities, and ultimately, what we call the Creator Economy. Call it Web 2.0.

With connectivity almost everywhere on the go and easily accessible internet, we are (or probably have) slowly and now swiftly paving the way for Web 3.0. A world that won't be regulated by apps, internet companies or dominant players. It is going to be a world that is decentralized, as omnipresent as oxygen, and a huge part of it will exist without devices. And much more, which only the future will unveil. Welcome to Web 3.0, my friend.

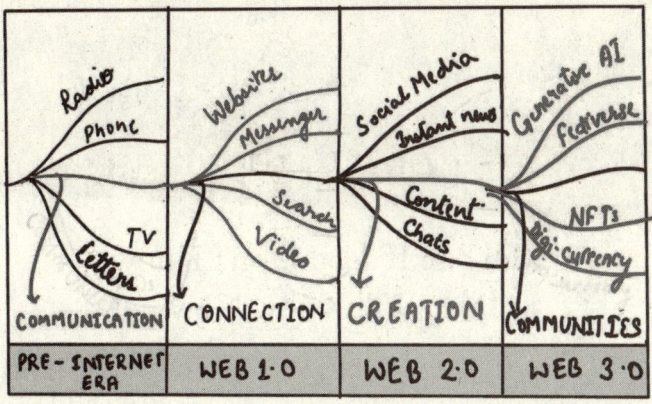

In the image: Web 1.0 is a subset of the pre-internet era, Web 2.0 is a subset of Web 1.0, Web 3.0 is a subset of Web 2.0, and so on.

Speaking of Web 2.0, which is still at its peak stage, the evolution of communication in the digital world led us to the omnipotent, omnipresent, and of course, omniscient Creator Economy.

As we step into the future, into Web 3.0, the Creator Economy is going to be nothing but filled with miracles, surprises, and most importantly, possibilities for each of the 5 pillars.

But before we dive deep in, time for a bit of awareness.

Key takeaways:

- The Creator Economy, as a revolution, has evolved through several years of small revolutions.
- Web 3.0 (which stands for communities) is a subset of Web 2.0 (which stands for creation), which is a subset of Web 1.0 (which stood for connection), and which was a subset of pre-internet era (which stood for communication).

Chapter 5(b)

Web 3.0: If You Don't Know, You Will Know Now

In the sense of awareness, this chapter is going to be filled with the latest developments in the space of the Creator Economy and where we are headed. However, by the time you hold this book in your hands, some of these developments may have already become obsolete and paved the way for newer ones.

Thus, my role is not to educate you on an exhaustive list of the latest stuff, but to show you how we got here, all that we have got till now, and give you a perspective to look at the new developments we are headed towards.

First things first: You don't need to get scared that these new advancements will take your job away. Computers did not take away manual jobs. If anything they exponentially created new jobs. However, the key is to learn, adapt and be acutely aware of the world we are living in, because that is the only way we can win in the Creator Economy.

I think it is important to take a quick glance at the multiple pillars of the future of content creation before we dive deep into the problems that lie ahead.

These elements, might I say, are going to become as ubiquitous as oxygen for the Web 3.0 world, thus affecting all the 5Cs in some way or the other.

Virtual Reality:

Virtual Reality is the concept where the user enters an entirely digital environment using a VR device, such as Oculus or Apple Vision Pro. These devices block out the physical world and the user is immersed in a simulated environment that reacts to the user's interactions.

Augmented Reality:

Augmented Reality is something that does not require a dedicated device to experience, and it superimposes digital content onto the real-world environment to enhance the viewing experience. For example, if you are ordering a burger at a restaurant, you are not just watching the 2D menu or the video representation on a device, you are also able to view the superimposed burger in 3D right in front of you and how it would look once you order it.

Metaverse:

Metaverse is a virtual shared space where users can interact with each other in virtual worlds. It is the universe where virtual reality takes place. There could be many parallel metaverses for e.g., social metaverse, gaming metaverse, education metaverse, etc.

Wise people always are wondering where the puck is going. Mark Zuckerberg is a stunning example of that. In October 2021, Facebook was renamed, and Zuckerberg rebranded its corporate identity to 'Meta'.

In addition to Meta, tech giants including Google, Microsoft, Nvidia and Qualcomm are also investing billions of dollars in the concept. Management consultancy McKinsey & Company has bullishly predicted that the metaverse economy could reach $5 trillion by 2030.[1]

Generative AI:

Another big revolution that is taking the internet by storm is Artificial Intelligence along with its leg of Large Language Models.

This is a specific way of simulating human intelligence in systems and developing algorithms to perform tasks that require human intelligence such as reasoning, coding, problem-solving, looking up information, decision-making based on data, etc.

Large Language Models are a subset of artificial intelligence that are trained on an infinite amount of text and data using deep learning techniques like neural networks to process and generate human language aka human-like text.

Fediverse:

Fediverse is like http or oxygen: it is around you, but probably not something most of us think about often.

Defined technically, Fediverse is an interconnected social platform ecosystem based on an open protocol called ActivityPub, which allows you to port your content, data and follower graph between networks.

Translated simply, Fediverse is a universe where you can take all your content and make them interoperable. Which means, you can post any content piece from anywhere, and all your followers across all platforms would be able to see it. Also, you could transfer all your followers with you if, at any point of time, you decide to quit any platform. A thirty-second elevator pitch is: You are the owner of your content and your audience, across all platforms.

Cryptocurrency:

Cryptocurrency is a decentralized method of payment on a blockchain platform. They are not controlled by any bank or government, but are on a large public ledger, also called Distributed Ledger Platform or the blockchain.

The first cryptocurrency was Bitcoin. However, as of June 2023, there were a total of more than 25,000 cryptocurrencies.

For example, the buying and selling of NFTs (Non-Fungible Tokens) is recorded on blockchain and is funded through one of the cryptocurrencies.

DeFi, or Decentralized Finance refers to financial services built on blockchain technology. Its function is to recreate and improve traditional financial systems (like lending, borrowing, trading, and insurance) in a decentralized manner, without relying on traditional banks or financial institutions.

To put it all together, DeFi (ecosystem) enables transactions on blockchain (technology) using cryptocurrencies—all in a decentralized manner.

...

These are a few terms such as AR, VR, Gen AI, etc. that Web 3.0 has generated so far. The future will certainly create more terms, and hence, the world is ready to expand and explode.

Which brings me back to the year 2004.

If you go back to 2004 and meet Mark Zuckerberg at Harvard and ask him about virtual reality in a metaverse, he will know nothing about it. (Or maybe *he* would)

But today, virtual reality is as real as the 'real' reality.

What I intend to say is that the above list of new developments that will drive the future of the Creator Economy is not exhaustive and the future developments are only going to surprise us.

However, I would also like to add, that with every peak, there is a valley. True for life, true for business, true for everything. The future of the Creator Economy, or Web 3.0, is no different. What would be the most useful (and would help each one of us thrive in the Web 3.0 world) is the right use of tech and understanding of the future of tech. This will only help us develop our own wisdom of growth and pursue it in a manner that is conducive to us.

Given that, at any point in time, each one of us is at one of the 5Cs of the Creator Economy.

It would be fun to explore how the future looks, for each of these 5Cs.

Key takeaways:

Here are some important elements that will define Web 3.0 (the list is non-exhaustive and will only grow over time):

Virtual Reality: The user enters an entirely different environment through the use of a VR device.

Augmented Reality: It is a superimposition of digital content to the real-world environment, sans the use of devices.

Metaverse: It is a virtual universe; a virtual shared space where users can interact with each other.

Generative AI: It is a specific way of simulating human intelligence in systems and developing algorithms to perform tasks that require human intelligence.

Fediverse: It is a universe where you can take all your content and make them interoperable, allowing you to post any content piece from anywhere, and all your followers across all platforms would be able to see it.

Cryptocurrency: Cryptocurrency is a decentralized method of payment (which is not controlled by any bank or government) that operates on a blockchain platform.

Chapter 5(c)

The 5Cs of the Creator Economy, for the Future

Okay, so you and I have spoken about the 5Cs of the Creator Economy in multiple ways throughout the book.

This time, we take a spin.

Of what could be. Because no one knows.

Creators:

AI has made life so much easier for creators. I would not say it is a 100 per cent replacement for a creator (at least, for now) who puts in 'their personality' in the content that they create, but AI subscription tools such as ChatGPT, Claude, Perplexity etc. for less than the cost of three pizzas a month is a revolution.

The game of creators in the future is not going to be the game that has played out till now—to follow a trend, do it better, while being yourself.

The game of the creator is going to be to do all the above in addition to being faster, cheaper and leveraging AI to bring exponential quality of content (and even quantity, when needed).

The economic moat of creators—defined by their uniqueness, personality, and personal touch—will be the previously replaceable staff who can leverage AI using the creator's voice to produce 10x better work.

The more a 'human' understands the person behind the creator, the more indispensable that creator becomes.

Channels:

The new channels that are being launched are finding it hard to compete with the established players. Even Threads (the competitor to Twitter (X) launched by Meta) did not live up to the hype it created. Well, it is the love child of Instagram (and Facebook) so no one knows where it will go eventually, though.

With Web 3.0 dominating the market and only the top companies such as Meta, Microsoft, Google, Apple, etc. having the resources to venture into making new devices (such as Apple Vision Pro, Quest by Meta), the power will be tilted and vested in the hands of the big players.

Or maybe the Fediverse could challenge this very concept.

In either case, this is an opportunity for tech start-ups to bring cost-effective yet hi-tech solutions to the market. The distribution of power to all has to begin with the visionaries thinking of using the power they have.

And if the regulatory bodies the world over don't want to show up late to the party (as in the current scenario where regulators are trying to catch up to the technological advancements in big tech), it is best to play an active role now. It will ensure that the powers of the future of social media are not (again) concentrated on a few players only. What seems like a threat is an opportunity for regulators. Because tech is moving faster than elections. To be able to meet the fast pace, regulators not only need to have oversight, but they also cannot ignore the absence of it. They should be more proactive. Be early. Have skin in the game.

Regulators should be friends or auditors or co-owners of the progress, not merely supporters or adopters or witnesses.

Consumer/Community:

The average mobile screen time increased by 30 per cent, from two hours and fifty-six minutes in 2019 to four hours and twelve minutes in 2021 and surged by a staggering 66 per cent in 2024, reaching six hours and fifty-eight minutes daily. This adds up to nearly forty-nine hours per week—equivalent to a total of 168 hours per month.[2]

This picture is a satire on our conditions as human beings—what do we even do if we have no screen time?!

This leads to not only app fatigue and inability to decide where to spend time, but also leads to deviated and distributed attention of the consumer. Thus, the views we think as views might possibly be mere sleepwalking.

On the flip side, what does it take to nurture communities? To build human-to-human bonds, democratize entertainment and education, create connectivity through holograms, host virtual concerts, among other things. However, there are also significant concerns: biological hazards, online trust and safety (for instance, a woman was molested in the metaverse), privacy issues and financial frauds enabled by AI.

It is going to be a challenge for all other 4Cs to nurture this 5th C in the most important manner. Consumer is the core pillar of the entire Creator Economy.

Collaborators (Brands):

The weird thing about collaborators is that to stay relevant, they have to create content in a way that resonates with the audience (gone are the days of 'this is our product, link in bio'). They have to serve first, sell later. Therefore, collaborators are becoming creators in their own way.

If that isn't all, with time, consistency, and engagement, creators are now becoming brands.

If I tell you MrBeast, Cocomelon and Jake Paul have launched their respective merchandise—just by hearing their names, you already have an idea of what the merchandise is going to be like.

Creators are becoming brands as they grow. For example, MrBeast has struck a deal with Amazon MGM Studios for his first ever TV series, touted as 'the biggest reality competition series in television history', where 1000 contestants compete for a $5 million cash payout. By the way, it is also the biggest single prize in the history of television and streaming.[3] In another instance, Dude Perfect, the five-member comedy and sports YouTube creator company, raised over $100 million, which they plan to use to flex their brand well beyond online videos.[4]

This is a difficult time for brands. Since the audience of almost all creators are different, they must define a thorough strategy before choosing to work with any creator.

But here is the good part for brands: If they can humanize their experience and establish themselves as creators, they are on the road to becoming timeless and loved forever. Brands humanizing the AI through their voice and tonality are eventually going to win.

Commerce:

The developing markets of the world—Brazil, South Asia, etc.—which weren't at the forefront during the peak of the social media revolution and evolution, will now drive consumerism by adopting and adapting ideas and innovations from developed markets. What is also interesting to see is how this will play out in the decentralized economy as Web 3.0 takes over.

The Challenges are huge.

But the opportunities in the future are way bigger.

…

All of this is what the moving parts of the Creator Economy (the 5Cs—Creators, Channels, Consumers, Collaborators, and Commerce) are assumed to become in the world we live in.

While there will be great developments to watch unfold, it would be truly incredible to listen to the subject matter experts, people who have been in the Creator Economy for decades, think about their view of the future in the next chapter.

Key takeaways:

Here is how Web 3.0 will impact the 5Cs of the Creator Economy:

Creators (C1): The creator's game will be to replicate everything they've already done—but faster, more cost-effectively, and by leveraging AI to exponentially enhance both the quality and the quantity of their content.

Channels (C2): With only trillion-dollar companies dominating the space, this an opportunity for tech start-ups to bring cost-effective yet hi-tech solutions to the market. Also, regulators should be friends (or auditors) of this progress, not merely supporters or adopters or witnesses.

Consumers (C3): What does it take to nurture communities? To build human to human bonds, to democratize entertainment, education, to create connectivity through holograms and have virtual concerts, among other things. It is the responsibility of the other 4Cs to understand how to replace growing screen time with 'real' time.

Collaborators (C4): If brands can humanize their experience and establish themselves as creators, they are on the road to becoming timeless and loved forever.

Commerce (C5): Developing markets will accelerate the growth of Web 3.0, primarily because of the sheer scale of adoption, which is the core of the Creator Economy.

Chapter 5(d)

What Experts Have to Say

As we've observed by now, the Creator Economy's impact on all of us has been made possible through both small and large contributions from people around the world.

Thus, as we talk about what the future of the Creator Economy will look like, I thought it would be a great idea to take an expert opinion from people who are top voices on the subject, and people whom I look up to, for their contributions and opinions in the Creator Economy space.

Here we go:

Phil Ranta

Phil Ranta is the chief operating officer of Fixated, a content and gaming studio building IP around creators, a LinkedIn top voice in innovation and technology and has been creating content for the internet and building internet businesses professionally for nearly twenty years, since his days on MySpace, and adopting trends till date. He was the Head of Gaming Creators, North America at Facebook, the first network lead at Fullscreen, the chief operating officer at Studio71, and spent ten years as a working comedian (including two years on cruise ships). He's a husband, a dad of two and (a self-proclaimed) insufferable digital media wonk.

Phil was generous enough to share his insights on generative AI, how communities are built, the human behaviour of upcoming generations, and of course, the ever present AI glasses.

He believes that generative AI video models will commoditize easily replicable, less creative content value propositions like attractive models, cute puppies, explainer videos and news. The creators that survive and thrive will lean into the one thing a computer can't re-create: personal stories.

When he says that, I find it quite incredible yet promising, because that is the core of the Creator Economy: to share our most authentic selves with the rest of the world.

Coming to conversations with the rest of the world, Phil has a unique take on building communities. He says, 'Communities are already built through games, and the next frontier will involve creator content built into games. Fortnite UEFN and Roblox are just the beginning. Soon, creators will be able to easily build and incentivize their community to join, compete, and win through custom-built gamified experiences.'

I think gamified communities are going to be the next big WOW thing, considering the audience wants more personalization and 'people like us' experience, and certainly not be in a place where they are just a fly on the wall.

This is specifically important for upcoming generations, as Ranta rightly says: 'Upcoming generations have even less tolerance for ads, so affiliate programmes and ads integrated into content are about to become even more powerful. Creators that can convert audiences will thrive. TikTok Shop sellers are tomorrow's e-commerce millionaires.'

I honestly can't wait for such a revolution to occur, because it gives the creators much-needed leverage for their work, and the audience a much-needed interface without ad interference. Then they have all the reason to fall in place together.

Which brings us to the long pending speculation on augmented reality glasses. Phil agrees and goes on to predict when they will finally become the present from the future.

'AR glasses are still, and always have been, the future mobile device. Now we are on the cusp of generative AI, quantum computing, and advancements in chip technology that will make this concept mainstream in the next five years.'

The rapid pace of change in the online world is evident. Even established platforms like Google Video, Yahoo! video, AOL and MySpace have faded. Phil, with his extensive experience, has witnessed this evolution first-hand. These online spaces do not exist any more. However, the fact that Phil not only stays relevant but continues to rise in his relevance is an endorsement to his deep understanding of the content ecosystem. Ignore his views at your own peril.

Meredith Levine

Meredith Levine is a full-time fanthropologist at Random Machine, where her work involves research, tracking and explaining internet culture and trends to help brands make better strategic decisions and recommendations for programming, marketing, content strategy, audience development and internal circulation of research. She brings years of experience exploring the big questions around building the future of entertainment in the attention economy, through custom research projects and strategic consulting.

Here are her hot takes:

Levine's deep insights into creators as culture carriers are worth their weight in gold. She goes on to say, 'Big, mega celebrities will have their own fan communities, with a layer of professional, or semi-professional fans that are known to the broader fandom. Many fans now will make content, products, and experiences for fellow fans. These celebrities carry and propagate distinct cultural identities and values—think how Swifties engage with other Swifties.'

How about short video creators? Levine says fandom is a difficult mountain to climb with short videos. She says, 'Fandom is hard to come by and it's even harder with short videos. Building authentic fandom will be increasingly challenging, especially for short-form video creators. The reason for that is that it is difficult for the community to engage with transient content creators. It lacks time spent building a relationship between the creator and their regular, returning audiences. Short-form creators are more likely to build audiences rather than true fandoms. They may capture attention but struggle to foster the deep cultural connections that characterize genuine fandom.'

I concur with her and think that it is fair play for creators who put in effort to make longer videos a viewing experience for their audience, as fandom and loyalty are earned through deeper connections.

Speaking of creators, Meredith says, 'Creators will evolve into lifestyle brands and will go on tours to create immersive experiences with their associated brands and for their niche target audiences.' This will be particularly relevant as the attention spans of people would continue to get shorter, and creators would live in an attention-first monetization-second world. She goes on to say, 'As the attention economy keeps fragmenting, the focus will be to capture attention first and then monetize through products, services and cultural touchpoints—a reversal of the traditional model (make a good product then figure out how to sell it).'

What is particularly insightful for me is how her thoughts about the future are constructive and optimistic and are full of possibilities for each one of us.

Speaking of possibilities, Meredith has a unique take on AI. 'Artificial intelligence and Creator Economy won't compete with each other, but rather complement each other. Creators who are serious about creating true fandom, will use AI for what it does best, playing a supporting role, such as creating thumbnails, editing, titling, and translation (subtitles and dubbing), etc. This will be so because true fandom speaks and builds relatability to Creators' true personalities and not machine-generated personas.' Speaking of translation, she suggests, 'AI will cut through geographies and will create language markets instead, such as that for Spanish or Hindi, thus transcending geographical boundaries. AI may emerge as a cultural conduit, breaking down barriers and democratizing access to diverse musical expression and content creation more broadly.'

She most certainly believes the music industry will be disrupted by AI as it is easier to disrupt in an era of highly electronic music. Prompt engineering for music, especially music that follows conventions of a specific genre, might see highly successful engineers as objects of fandom.

With overall focus on fandom and how there is an arena of possibilities for creators in the future, Meredith's takes are invaluable if you want to create an audience that stands the test of time.

Jim Louderback

Jim Louderback is among the most respected figures in digital media with a twenty-five-year history of leadership at the intersection of media, video, content and technology. He successfully built and sold two start-ups to top media companies, hosted and organized hundreds of sessions and events, and has a proven track record of creating innovative companies that capitalize on what's 'around the corner'.

He has built and sold multiple Creator Economy start-ups to top media companies, including Discovery and Paramount.

Jim writes the popular weekly newsletter 'Inside the Creator Economy' on LinkedIn. Boasting over 30,000 subscribers, here are his short and to the point hot takes on the future of the Creator Economy:

Louderback contends creators are the future of sports, education, of TV, and of companies. (Fun fact: 26 per cent of social users are creators/influencers; and 10–15 per cent of people in a company are creators).

His 'Wacky' (as he calls them) predictions:

- A creator will win an Oscar by 2028.
- A VTuber or AI creator will be among the top 100 creators in 2025.
- A true middle class of creators will take 10 more years to develop.
- AI tools can replace 25 per cent of core business functions in three years.
- Subscription will never be a scale business for a larger segment of creators.
- Advertisers will start doing long-term multi-year sponsorships with creators—such as in sports.
- Creator brand deals and integrations will be transacted programmatically in three years.
- Companies develop unique bonus structures for employees who are also TikTokers.
- Media rooms get replaced by 'presence' rooms in upscale homes globally.
- MrBeast unseats Tom Tillis and is elected to the US Senate in 2026, or Mark Zuckerberg runs for President of the United States in 2032.

Even though Jim calls these 'Wacky' predictions, I think there is a lot of substance in them. Even if they seem outlandish for now, I believe a lot of them are on the cards to come to life. We see tinges and traces of almost every one of these in our lives today, and it will only be interesting to see how the clay moulds itself into a sculpture, eventually.

Saurabh Doshi

Saurabh held key leadership roles over two decades of his career and is passionate about the evolution of new technology, having played a pivotal role in several transitions—Web 2.0, mobile, video, social, and Creator Economy. He is now building the infrastructure blocks for blockchain and AI as a co-founder of Virtualness.

Saurabh has raised $10 million in funding for Virtualness and is building it at Stanford University campus along with other super smart founders from across the world.

He held senior roles at Meta for nearly a decade, heading Emerging Markets for Creator Products and Partnerships, as well as Managing Director Asia-Pacific, leading all entertainment experiences on Facebook and Instagram. Before Meta, Saurabh was Vice President and Business Head at Viacom Group overseeing digital initiatives for Star India and an investment banker with Bank of America. Saurabh has worked across geographies managing large teams as well as several products which went on to be used by over a billion users.

When speaking about what he thinks about the future of the Creator Economy, Saurabh says: 'AI has simplified the lives of creators by improving content distribution, personalization, targeting, and even managing IP, monetization, and smart contracts to enforce rights. In many cases, AI is also handling fan interactions and flagging negative content. It seems AI is becoming a natural co-pilot for creators, blending human creativity with machine efficiency to produce remarkable results.' He wonders if this is all real. Which is when he implores us to also consider the repercussions of AI. While it holds great potential to help the Creator Economy thrive and has a profound positive impact, we must also ensure full transparency so that end consumers know who they are engaging with and can make informed choices. The next generation is deeply immersed in technology and virtual environments, with a short attention span driven by short-form content. The risk of losing human touch is a reality we need to prevent.

Oh, by the way, what makes me the most hopeful is how Saurabh concludes his contention:

'This article is my original work and was not written by AI, though it did help with editing.' The fact that we need Saurabh's expertise and peek into the future is what perhaps will balance AI and human intelligence.

John Carle:

With over a decade in digital content, Carle says he has experienced lifetimes in the creator space. Whether it was being a creator's sole representation, leading high contributing talent facing teams or guiding brands through their first (or one hundred and first) campaign, he has maintained one goal across it all: empower creators to do what they do best and keep making content that their audiences love.

Here are his hot takes:

Regarding Artificial Intelligence, Carle says, 'These are early days in AI adoption and many creators are experimenting with AI to create content. This AI-generated content is easily identifiable, especially to the discerning eye. However, this trend will slowly shift in the future and AI would play a "supporting" role rather than a "creator role". Let's use machine learning to work on the parts of content creation that can provide efficiency and scale such as improved analytic analysis and insights or metadata creation.'

Carle discusses the future of content creation, arguing, the creator equivalent of mom & pop studios will become more central and ubiquitous. Sophisticated studios with high content creation costs will become unviable and the focus will shift to content studios that focus on making creative content even if the production quality has a little bit of the 'grit' that YouTube, Twitch and others are known for. This upper middle tier will have an understanding of what works best for digital native viewers because they are both the consumer and the contemporary to other creators. It won't feel like traditional media trying to make content for digital platforms.'

His advice to creators echoes Warren Buffett's classic principle: 'Don't put all your eggs in the same basket'. Carle says, 'Eventually, there will be fatigue for the current crowdfunded platform model. Like all things in digital, creators will need to ideate and iterate to prevent their audience from churning over time and find new reasons for someone to hop into their highest tier of fandom via payment. Creators that are primarily dependent on crowdfunded platforms as their primary (or only) revenue source should also seek to diversify their income streams as larger macro trends, like a recession, will quickly impact disposable income being donated to content creators.'

This is great advice to recession-proof yourself as a creator. Further, with regard to industry events, John opines that 'meaningful growth and change via industry gatherings lies in niche-focused "Speciality Conventions". Imagine intimate events with curated speakers, targeted discussions, and real networking opportunities. This shift will prioritize quality over quantity, delivering a more valuable experience for all stakeholders.'

Overall, John is an advocate for leveraging AI for what it does best, making creators do better and different from what they were already best at, and creating specialized experiences for the audience. As far as I am concerned, I couldn't agree more!

Avi Gandhi

Avi Gandhi writes about the business of creators on LinkedIn and through his newsletter with over 8,000 subscribers, Creator Logic. His consulting firm, Partner with Creators, provides go-to-market strategy and execution to businesses seeking to work with creators. He is also an advisor to the consumer team at Point72 Ventures. Over a fifteen-year career in digital media, Avi pioneered creator representation at Hollywood talent agency William Morris Endeavor, built an award-winning content production and management company for Jimmy Kimmel's Wheelhouse and led the Creator Partnerships team at Creator Economy unicorn, Patreon.

Avi's hot takes suggest AI will revolutionize every aspect of content creation. In his own words, 'AI is set to revolutionize content creation, potentially increasing the volume of available content by 10x, 100x, or even 1000x. This surge will ignite a battle between AI platforms and content algorithms (something like we've seen between the spam filters and the email marketers).' As a result, what will happen is 'while AI will get increasingly sophisticated and make more realistic content, algorithms will aim to identify and isolate AI-generated content. This tension will create a constant back & forth.'

Gandhi is nevertheless quite hopeful and very bullish on AI. He says, 'Despite this, AI will still continue to generate content at scale and skilled prompt engineering input will eventually result in good content output. Consequently, AI will increase the baseline quality expectations for all content.'

But what about human-made content? Is it going to be 100 per cent irrelevant? Avi has quite a deep take on this too: 'In this content clutter, however, human-made content will bring in a premium. For instance, consider the suit market—a factory can make thousands of good quality suits, increasing the quality level of suits in the market. As a result, there will be no demand for mediocre tailors. However, simultaneously, it will create opportunities for exceptional quality tailors who could command premium prices for their limited, hand-crafted suits.'

I believe this could be fantastic news for content creators who genuinely care about their work and consistently produce premium, value-driven content.

Because let's admit it, with AI being able to create content at scale, almost everyone will be a creator. Thus, it will also change the creative landscape from what it is today.

In Avi's words, 'AI's democratization of content creation will fundamentally alter the creative landscape. It will enable anyone to make content because of the sheer ease of content creation, thus levelling the playing field. This shift will be the converse of today's world. Traditional content creation skills will matter less in the future. The grind of content creation itself will be replaced by AI.'

So, what will eventually decide the success of the creator? Avi says, 'Success will depend more on the taste and vision of the creator and less on the creative process itself. As AI becomes more mainstream, a Curator Economy will rise alongside the Creator Economy.'

Hmm, a Curator Economy along with the Creator Economy. That would be an interesting space to watch.

Speaking of interesting spaces, Avi's views on product design and its impact on creators are also quite insightful. He says, 'Product design will become a much easier and accessible skill thanks to AI. This will enable creators to design and produce their own product lines without the need to find partners, raise funding, or hire teams. As a result, creators will evolve into small scale businesses by themselves.'

I think this is a much-awaited development the world needs from creators. Since the creator would have to go through lesser pain and would be able to develop better, deeper products, it is only a boon for every creator.

Avi also cites an example, 'For instance, a lifestyle creator who reviews furniture would be able to leverage AI to create their own sofa design, generate the necessary 3D models for factories to produce it, and create the marketing materials to sell to their audience, thereby reducing the need for partnerships and hiring.'

However, what is the overall impact of this?

'This shift will help creators expand their economic dominance into other areas of the economy—beyond just marketing tools for companies, they will become the product creators and sellers themselves. Moreover, this fusion of creative vision with AI-powered design tools could result in novel products that resonate deeply with niche audiences.'

Isn't that amazing? For all the work that the creators before us have done to take the Creator Economy to this level, they fully deserve to create their own economy using AI.

I'm all eyes on this prediction!

Ankur Mehra (Yours Truly)

The content creation strategy, as the veterans of the Creator Economy world would know, is broadly divided into three types—Hero, Hub and Hygiene.

Hero content is high-impact, attention-grabbing content.

Hub content is regular recurring content, designed to increase brand awareness and build trust.

Hygiene content is evergreen foundational content, to keep your business cycle running.

Generative AI will end up integrating deeply into the content generation lifecycle. What this means is that AI will not only be used for mundane tasks such as editing, thumbnail designs etc., but will also be used in a much more integrated manner.

In other words, while AI will be primarily and wholly used for Hygiene content, it will also be used for co-creation in Hub content, and very sparingly used for creating Hero content.

It is the Hero content that will be creator-driven, with personal touch, emotions, learnings, thinking, etc., and will drive subscription (pay-per-view), while the rest will be ad-driven.

When it comes to fan engagement, AI creator-mirror bots will be used to interact with fans on the basic day-to-day inbounds. However, for more nuanced interactions, such as curated behind-the-scenes, mentoring, creator meet-greet, etc., the creator will lead the audience engagement behind the paywall, using a subscription-based model.

With respect to marketing tech agencies, they will evolve their business models from the current AI matchmaking and dashboard metrics to providing deep and more nuanced value to their brand clients. The leading agencies will start to cater to start-ups and medium-sized businesses, instead of the big global companies (as is the case now) since a large part of the marketing dollars will come from these enterprises.

Speaking of the economic shift of balance, we will see small and medium businesses starting to engage at scale with emerging and aspiring creators. Reminding you of the lower left quadrant in the brand—creator matrix in Chapter 4. Resharing the diagram below

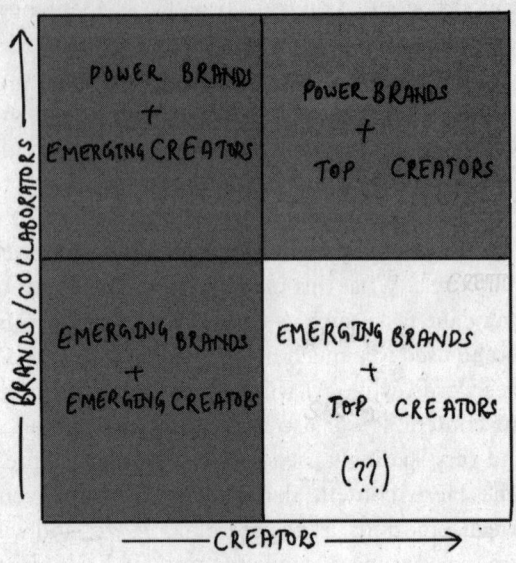

...

To sign off, isn't it incredible that all of us have a positive, more focused, optimistic view of the future, yet all of us are thinking on entirely different tangents?

The real race isn't about whose insights will come true—they all will, eventually. The question is: when they do, will we be ready to adapt?

For that, let me take you to my childhood in the following chapter.

Key takeaways:

Phil Ranta:

Phil Ranta, chief operating officer of Fixated and digital media expert, shares insights on AI's impact on content creation, emphasizing the importance of personal stories. He predicts gamified communities will dominate, affiliate marketing will grow, and AR glasses will become mainstream within five years.

Meredith Levine:

Meredith Levine, a celebrated fanthropologist, offers insights on internet culture trends. She discusses the evolution of fandom, challenges for short-form creators, and the future of the Creator Economy. Levine predicts AI will complement creators, potentially disrupt music, and facilitate cross-cultural content sharing while stressing on the importance of authentic connections in building lasting audiences.

Jim Louderback:

Jim Louderback, a respected digital media leader with over twenty-five years of experience, shares his wacky predictions on the Creator Economy's future. His predictions include the impact of creators on various industries, AI's integration, changes in advertising models and potential shifts in politics and home design.

Saurabh Doshi:

Saurabh Doshi, a tech veteran and co-founder of Virtualness, sees AI as a co-pilot for creators, enhancing content distribution, personalization, and management. However, he also believes we have a dire need for transparency of use of AI and maintaining human touch along with these AI advancements, especially considering the next generation's tech-immersed lifestyle and the repercussions it brings along.

John Carle:

John Carle, a digital content veteran, predicts AI will shift to a supporting role in content creation, foresees the rise of 'Mom & Pop' content studios, advises creators to diversify income streams, and anticipates a trend towards niche-focused industry events. Carle is bullish at creating specialized audience experiences.

Avi Gandhi:

Avi Gandhi, a digital media expert, predicts AI will dramatically increase content volume and make creation easier for everyone. He believes human-made content will become premium, and success will depend on creators' taste rather than technical skills. Gandhi foresees a 'Curator Economy' emerging and AI helping creators design their own products, potentially turning them into small businesses.

Ankur Mehra:

In the Hero-Hub-Hygiene model, I believe AI will be primarily used for Hygiene content, co-creating Hub content, and minimally for Hero content. AI bots will handle basic fan interactions, while creators lead paid, nuanced engagements. Marketing agencies will evolve to provide deeper value.

Chapter 5(e)

From the Past to the Present, into the Future

I belong to the luckiest generation in the history of civilization. And the luckiest generation that ever will be.

Okay, before you judge, hear me out: Yes, I was not born with a smartphone in my hand. I did not spend my teenage years on Bumble and Tinder. (Because they did not exist at the time.)

I did not grow up in an era where an AI tool would design graphics for me or suggest recipes for a weekend the rare chef inside me wanted to cook.

However, that is exactly the point.

My generation has seen technology advancing from its embryonic stage to its empirical stage today.

I have witnessed first-hand the internet.

Okay, let me share a great contrast:

I watched my first movie in a movie theatre at fifteen years of age.

My son watched his first movie in a multiplex—not a single-screen theatre—at just fifteen months old.

My son and I are twenty-nine years apart.

I find it both fascinating and strange how our collective consciousness as content consumers is evolving, yet most of what we consume today didn't exist in this form just a few years ago.

How did this happen?

How did we get to a place where we have everything at our fingertips and every content at the tangent of our thought, from a time of letters, postcards, inland letters and radios?

I was born in the 'electricity era'. We had outages, but there were working fans, lights and coolers (not ACs, like most of us do today).

When my son opened his eyes, he always had the internet. When he was born, there was internet on our smartphones, not just on desktops and laptops. The internet was not a new phenomenon, it was a common phenomenon. I'd say my son was born in the 'internet era'.

When my son has his own kids, they will already be born in the Metaverse. It won't be a cool new thing; it would rather be a given.

That is why I believe I belong to the luckiest generation— one that witnessed the advent of the internet, its evolution into countless subsets, and its continued growth.

What I do know for sure is wherever you and I are, we are ready to witness a massive transformation over the next five to ten years.

Wherever you are, you are at the cusp of transformation.

The good news is that whether or not you ride that wave isn't entirely up to you.

I may not have ridden the wave of internet transformation, nor would I be writing this book to you on a subject I'm deeply passionate about, but the internet would still be a part of whatever I do, regardless of my background.

The same is perhaps true for each one of us.

So, the future, I figure, is what one of the most inspirational people on the planet once quoted: Stay hungry, stay foolish.

Might I take the liberty to add: Stay curious and have some fun with the future as we blend it into our present.

Key takeaways:

- My generation has witnessed the evolution of technology from its early stages to today. While I didn't grow up with smartphones or AI, I saw the internet's rise, and my son was born into an internet-dominated world.
- The changes in lifestyles through generations, like my son experiencing a movie theatre at fifteen months compared to my first at fifteen years, are a small glance into the superfast speed innovation that lies before us as we move forward.
- Future generations will likely be born into the Metaverse, and while we don't know what's next, we all are always at the cusp of another transformation.
- Staying curious and open to change is a fun mindset to have, as the future blends into our present lives.

Epilogue

I was born in a military hospital in Palampur, a city in the northern part of India, and since have been raised in over ten cities across the country.

My father was an officer in the Indian Army, and he frequently got posted to different parts of the country.

Thus, throughout my childhood, I had the proud privilege of growing up in lush, green and clean military cantonments. By the time I was in my teens, it was clear as daylight that I would go on to join the Army. Just like my father.

Anyone even remotely connected with me knew that I would join the Army. My friends, acquaintances, extended family, even friends of friends.

Sure enough, I did.

After completing a gruelling training in the Indian Military Academy for 18 months, I joined my elite regiment in the formidable Corps of Artillery of the Indian Army. For the uninitiated, the Corps of Artillery is responsible for providing fire power support to other arms in combat operations.

I served in the Army for seven years, the absolute highlight of my life's story.

These formative years shaped me forever. This is where I made friends—no, brothers—for life. In the short span of time that I was in the Army, I was posted from the dry and unforgiving sand dunes of Rajasthan to the chilly and dizzying heights of Jammu and Kashmir.

Life in the Army is something else. It is not a profession. It is a way of life. However, life had different plans.

After serving seven proud years, I was posted in Delhi.

At the time, the capital city and its neighbouring city, Gurgaon (now called Gurugram), were transforming into sprawling megacities—futuristic, IT-enabled hubs.

The world was changing right in front of my eyes, and I felt excited (and nervous) about my second innings in the corporate sector.

Thus, as is characteristically me, who would check the depth of the pool after stepping into it, I landed myself into the corporate world (did I tell you I am a pro swimmer?) with not even an iota of understanding of what to expect there.

You see, since the day I was born (remember—military hospital), I had never ever been in civilian environs. This was unfamiliar territory to me.

However, over the past sixteen years, I have been blessed to be associated with the largest network conglomerate in India to working with one of the top ten most valuable companies of the world; from working in the poshest offices to walking the lanes of the largest slums in the world; from meeting the celebrities I would once watch on *Chitrahaar* in the large box TV in our home to seeing creators go from rags to riches through virtue of their hard work and persistence.

The military experience wasn't less colourful in any way.

Sometimes, the bonds forged in the Army with our brothers-in-arms are even stronger than the ones we have with our biological families. I formed the best friendships of my life in the field and unfortunately lost some true warriors who made the ultimate sacrifice in the line of duty. Fallen heroes whose memories I'll honour forever.

I had the privilege of serving my country for years, and I am proud I get to call myself a *fauji* (soldier) till I die.

However, as I sit back on my balcony sometimes, sipping my black pour over coffee thinking about my career journey, a lot that panned out was never planned that way.

I had little or no role to play in it, other than to go with the flow. I certainly never made a vision board of working in the military or delivering a presentation at a conference.

It just happened.

Much like the Creator Economy.

Susan Wojcicki didn't rent out her garage to start Google just to pay her mortgage; she did it because she was excited by what Larry Page and Sergey Brin were building, even though the company had few users and zero revenue.[1]

Mark Zuckerberg did not drop out of Harvard and get bailed out by his parents because he showed them what the Creator Economy could do.

Khaby Lame did not record wordless videos sitting at his home in Italy to become the 'world's most followed TikToker'.

The Creator Economy evolved over the years, perhaps centuries, to create a revolution we all live in today.

And here we are.

With almost every business, every individual and every celebrity hoping to become a creator.

Having known and worked with a lot of them, no one has some concrete five-year or even a three-year plan, because the industry is so agile.

However, the best of the best creators, that I have had the privilege to know, have a relentless obsession with their brand and are passionate about what they do. The book you are holding in your hands is a by-product of my obsession with the Creator Economy, which the teenage Ankur living in a small town would have never thought about.

It just happened as a by-product of my passion for the Creator Economy

So, my friend, if you are sitting on the fence wondering if the Creator Economy is for you, or if you should build a content-based brand around yourself or your business, maybe the thought itself is an answer to your question.

If you are still unsure, just lead with passion.

As we sign off, please also know that I have been that person all my career, and in the process of 'it just happened' and going with the flow, I have almost always happened to find my flow.

Maybe you will too.

I don't know of anyone who hasn't.

Acknowledgements

I vividly remember that day. It was pouring (as it normally does) in Singapore, I was catching up on life and work with Neha, a very dear friend, and was telling her how my book (yes, the one you're holding right now) was shaping up, when she half-jokingly and half-seriously said, 'You joined the army because that's your dad's legacy (he was an army officer), but you became an author thanks to your mom's genes (she was a schoolteacher)'. This was truly a light bulb moment for me. As I reflect on my journey, I realize that there couldn't have been a more fitting reflection of my life and career path.

So, thank you, dad (I'm sure you are in a better place), for being the role model that you were and will always continue to be! I miss you.

Thank you, mom, for passing down those academic genes that we kept searching for during my academic years. Well, here they are now.

Thank you, Inks, my growing up partner-in-crime! Remember when we thought adulthood would be all fun and no responsibility? Good times.

To Vibhank, my son, thank you for being my greatest teacher, my toughest critic, my biggest fan and . . . my favourite person.

Thank you, Vibha, for being the constant in Vibhank's life and raising him with such dedication and care.

While I am grateful to be surrounded by many friends and well-wishers, I will particularly call out Neha for being a huge supporter through the life journey of this book.

Rachna for believing in the promise and potential of this book. And my dear military mates Parti and Katy—it's been an honour (and 'occasionally' a pleasure) growing up with you!

This book wouldn't exist without my wonderful editors Radhika, Sakshi, Aninda, Naina, Bhavika and the entire team at Penguin Random House, along with Mohit and Tanuf from Paper Sparrows, and Preeti from Sunflower Seeds. Thank you for believing in this project and helping to bring it to life.

And to you, dear reader, thank you for being the final piece of this puzzle. As you can see, it took a village to bring this book together.

Notes

Foreword

1 'The Creator Economy Could Approach Half a Trillion Dollars by 2027', *Goldman Sachs Insights*, 2023, https://www.goldmansachs.com/insights/articles/the-creator-economy-could-approach-half-a-trillion-dollars-by-2027.html

Preface

1 'Adobe Future of Creativity Study: 165M+ Creators Joined Creator Economy Since 2020', *Adobe News*, 2022, https://news.adobe.com/news/news-details/2022/Adobe-Future-of-Creativity-Study-165M-Creators-Joined-Creator-Economy-Since-2020/default.aspx

The 5C Framework of the Creator Economy

1 'The creator economy could approach half-a-trillion dollars by 2027', *Goldman Sachs Insights*, 2023, https://www.goldmansachs.com/insights/articles/the-creator-economy-could-approach-half-a-trillion-dollars-by-2027.html

Chapter 1: The First and the Foremost

1 'Television Replaced Radio as the Dominant Medium, with 50 Million Households Having Them by 1960', Elon University *Imagining Time Capsule*, 2023, https://www.elon.edu/u/imagining/

time-capsule/150-years/back-1920-1960/%23:~:text=Televi
sion%252520replaced%252520radio%252520as%252520the,
million%252520had%252520them%252520by%2525201960.

2 'Back 1920-1960', *Imagining the Internet*, 2025, https://www.elon.
edu/u/imagining/time-capsule/150-years/back-1920-1960/

3 'Apollo 11 Moon Landing', *National Air and Space Museum*, 2025,
https://airandspace.si.edu/explore/stories/apollo-11-moon-
landing/

4 Facebook was located out of Palo Alto in 2006; at the time of
the launch of Facebook video, however, in 2012, Facebook
headquarters moved to Menlo Park, California, which is where
the current headquarters of the company (now Meta) are located.
Source: https://en.wikipedia.org/wiki/Facebook?

5 'Instagram statistics', *Business of Apps*, https://www.
businessofapps.com/data/instagram-statistics/.

6 'Ed Sheeran's "Shape of You"', *New York Times*, 20 December
2017, https://www.nytimes.com/interactive/2017/12/20/arts/
music/ed-sheeran-shape-of-you.html.

7 'Charlie Bit My Finger NFT auction', *New York Times*, 24 May
2021, https://www.nytimes.com/2021/05/24/arts/charlie-bit-
my-finger-nft-auction.html.

8 'North Face's reaction to NZ jacket complaint goes viral', *Otago
Daily Times*, 2025, https://www.odt.co.nz/regions/queenstown/
north-faces-reaction-nz-jacket-complaint-goes-viral/

9 'TV technician's influencer daughter dazzles at Cannes', *Times of India*,
https://timesofindia.indiatimes.com/city/meerut/tv-technicians-
influencer-daughter-dazzles-at-cannes/articleshow/110294713.
cms.

Chapter 2: Globalization of Content

1 https://x.com/mufaddal_vohra/status/1809508792180015571

2 https://x.com/mufaddal_vohra/status/1809500469217124363

3 https://x.com/mufaddal_vohra/status/1809171795028684996

4 https://youtu.be/UVcJ-jaJkGo

5   'Adobe Future of Creativity Study: 165M+ Creators Joined
    Creator Economy Since 2020', *Adobe News*, 2022, https://news.
    adobe.com/news/news-details/2022/adobe-future-of-creativity-
    study-165m-creators-joined-creator-economy-since-2020.

6   'Future of Creativity Study: Creators in the Creator Economy',
    Adobe, 2022, https://s23.q4cdn.com/979560357/files/Adobe-
    'Future-of-Creativity'-Study_Creators-in-the-Creator-Economy.
    pdf.

7   'Not just content creators any more: how india's influencers
    are expanding their horizons', *Exchange4Media*, 2022, https://
    www.exchange4media.com/digital-news/not-just-content-
    creators-any more-how-indias-influencers-are-expanding-their-
    horizons-124052.html.

8   'Future of Creativity Study: Creators in the Creator Economy', *Adobe*,
    2022, https://s23.q4cdn.com/979560357/files/Adobe-'Future-of-
    Creativity'-Study_Creators-in-the-Creator-Economy.pdf.

9   L. Caldwell, 'I took a ride on the 'Swiftie Express' to see Taylor
    Swift in Santa Clara', *SFGate*, 2023, https://www.sfgate.com/
    sf-culture/article/swiftie-express-taylor-swift-santa-clara-eras-
    tour-18270916.php.

10 'Why people love Taylor Swift', *Medium*, 2025, https://
    preciousoladimeji.medium.com/why-people-love-taylor-swift-
    e59a4ccf6859/

11 'Cultural impact of Taylor Swift', Wikipedia, 2024, https://
    en.wikipedia.org/wiki/Cultural_impact_of_Taylor_Swift

12 'Taylor Swift's The Eras Tour Is Intimate, Colossal, and Slightly
    Disappointing', *New Yorker*, 2024, https://www.newyorker.com/
    culture/the-front-row/taylor-swift-the-eras-tour-is-intimate-
    colossal-and-slightly-disappointing

13 'About', *The Blog of Seth Godin*, 2024, https://seths.blog/about/

14 'People Like Us Do Stuff Like This', *The Blog of Seth Godin*, 2013,
    https://seths.blog/2013/07/people-like-us-do-stuff-like-this/

15 'George Floyd Investigation: What We Know So Far', *New York
    Times*, May 31, 2020, https://www.nytimes.com/2020/05/31/us/
    george-floyd-investigation.html.

16   'Teen Who Shot Cellphone Video of George Floyd Murder Gets Special Pulitzer Citation in Thumbs-Up to Citizen Journalism', *Times of India*, May 6, 2020, https://timesofindia.indiatimes.com/world/us/teen-who-shot-cellphone-video-of-george-floyd-murder-gets-special-pulitzer-citation-in-thumbs-up-to-citizen-journalism/articleshow/83462451.cms.

17   'Pulitzer Prize', *University of Washington*, 2025, https://www.washington.edu/research/or/honors-and-awards/pulitzer-prize/#:~:text=The%20Pulitzer%20Prize%20is%20regarded,yearly%20in%20twenty%2Done%20categories.

18   'The Fall of the Twin Towers and the Rise of Citizen Journalism', *Arapahoe News*, 11 September 2021, https://arapahoenews.com/15286/uncategorized/the-fall-of-the-twin-towers-and-the-rise-of-citizen-journalism/.

19   'How George Floyd's Murder Impacted Journalism in the United States', *World Press Institute*, May 25, 2020, https://worldpressinstitute.org/how-george-floyds-murder-impacted-journalism-in-the-united-states/.

Chapter 3: Democratization of Content

1   'India's Gangavva, a YouTube star at 60, shows the power of social media,' *CNN*, 19 August 2020, https://edition.cnn.com/2020/08/19/asia/india-youtube-star-gangavva-spc-intl/index.html.

2   'Adobe Future of Creativity Study: 165M+ Creators Joined the Creator Economy Since 2020,' *Adobe News*, 2022 bit.ly/3ZPI6UJ

3   'Who the F*ck Did I Marry?' *The Cut*, 2024, https://www.thecut.com/article/reesa-teesa-who-tf-did-i-marry-interview.html.

4   'The Different Types of Influencers: How & When to Leverage Their Reach,' *McSaatchi Performance*, 2024, https://www.mcsaatchiperformance.com/news/the-different-types-of-influencers-how-when-to-leverage-their-reach/.

5   'Influencer or creator? Here's how marketers can know who to hire', *Digiday*, accessed July 2024, https://digiday.com/marketing/

influencer-or-creator-heres-how-marketers-can-know-who-to-hire/.

6   'The Creator Economy Could Approach Half a Trillion Dollars by 2027', *Goldman Sachs*, https://www.goldmansachs.com/insights/articles/the-creator-economy-could-approach-half-a-trillion-dollars-by-2027.html.

7   'Adobe Future of Creativity Study: 165M+ Creators Joined Creator Economy Since 2020', *Adobe News*, https://news.adobe.com/news/news-details/2022/adobe-future-of-creativity-study-165m-creators-joined-creator-economy-since-2020.

8   'LinkedIn Update', *LinkedIn*, https://www.linkedin.com/feed/update/urn:li:activity:7188644915881340928/?originTrackingId=SlcxFbJAS/+QayB8d+EFYg==.

9   'The Marketing Rule of 7', *Marketing Illumination*, https://www.marketingillumination.com/blogs/marketing-rule-of-7s

10 'Purchase Funnel', *Wikipedia*, https://en.wikipedia.org/wiki/Purchase_funnel.

11 '95/5 Rule', *Marketing Week*, https://www.marketingweek.com/peter-weinberg-jon-lombardo-95-5-rule/.

12 'Does Influencer Marketing Really Pay Off?', *Harvard Business Review*, https://hbr.org/2022/11/does-influencer-marketing-really-pay-off.

13 'How YouTuber Prajakta Koli made it to the Paris Olympics', *LiveMint*, 2024, https://www.livemint.com/sports/how-youtuber-prajakta-koli-made-it-to-the-paris-olympics-11723300776834.html.

14 Youngest Indian billionaire in *Forbes* list is a school dropout. He shares the biggest moment of his life', *Economic Times*, 2024, https://economictimes.indiatimes.com/news/india/youngest-indian-billionaire-in-forbes-list-is-a-school-dropout-he-shares-the-biggest-moment-in-his-life/articleshow/109006210.cms?utm_source=contentofinterest&utm_medium=text&utm_campaign=cppst

15 'What Happened to Blackberry', *Toptal*, 2025, https://www.toptal.com/finance/management-consultants/what-happened-to-blackberry

16 'MBrandolph on Adaptability in Business,' *X*, 2024, https://x. com/mbrandolph/status/1610707460821749761. (Tweet).

17 'What Happened to Blackberry', *Toptal*, 2025, https://www. toptal.com/finance/management-consultants/what-happened-to-blackberry

18 'Unplugging for Your Mental Health', *Calgary Counselling Centre*, 2025, https://calgarycounselling.com/blog/unplugging-for-your-mental-health

19 'ONDC Explained: What is ONDC and How to Place an Order', *Paytm*, 2025, https://paytm.com/blog/ondc/ondc-explained-what-is-ondc-and-how-to-place-an-order/

Chapter 4: My Money Don't Jiggle Jiggle, It Folds—in the Creator Economy

1 'Adobe Future of Creativity Study: 165M+ Creators Joined Creator Economy Since 2020', *Adobe News*, 2022, https://news. adobe.com/news/news-details/2022/adobe-future-of-creativity-study-165m-creators-joined-creator-economy-since-2020

2 'MrBeast: Jimmy Donaldson', *TIME*, 2023, https://time.com/ collection/100-most-influential-people-2023/6270005/mrbeast-jimmy-donaldson/

3 'The Five Pillars Of Building Successfully In The Creator Economy', *Forbes*, 2023, https://www.forbes.com/councils/ forbesbusinesscouncil/2023/08/21/the-five-pillars-of-building-successfully-in-the-creator-economy/

4 'GroupM Releases its This Year Next Year 2024 Midyear Global Advertising Forecast', *GroupM*, 2024, https://www.groupm. com/newsroom/groupm-releases-its-this-year-next-year-2024-midyear-global-advertising-forecast/

5 'The Changing Landscape of Indian Television', *GroupM*, 2025, https:// www.groupm.com/the-changing-landscape-of-indian-television/

6 'Influencer Marketing Benefits', *Dash*, https://www.dash.app/ blog/influencer-marketing-benefits

7   'Roger Federer's Big Bet with On Is Paying Off', *Complex*, https://www.complex.com/sneakers/a/matt-welty/roger-federers-big-bet-with-on-is-paying-off

8   '5 Research-Backed Ways Creators Can Stand Out When Pitching Brands', *Impact*, 2025, https://impact.com/influencer/5-research-backed-ways-creators-can-stand-out-when-pitching-brands/

9   'How and why to maximize your creator marketing investment', *The Drum*, accessed date, https://www.thedrum.com/open-mic/how-and-why-to-maximize-your-creator-marketing-investment.

10   'The rule of 7: The power of social media', *Factorial HR*, 2025, https://factorialhr.com/blog/the-rule-of-7/

11   'About', *Creator Network*, https://creatornetwork.kit.com/about.

12   'Mental Health Disorder Statistics', *Johns Hopkins Medicine*, 2025, https://www.hopkinsmedicine.org/health/wellness-and-prevention/mental-health-disorder-statistics

13   'Data & Research on Diabetes', *Centers for Disease Control and Prevention (CDC)*, https://www.cdc.gov/diabetes/php/data-research/index.html

Chapter 5: The Future of the Creator Economy

1   'Value Creation in the Metaverse', *McKinsey & Company*, https://www.mckinsey.com/capabilities/growth-marketing-and-sales/our-insights/value-creation-in-the-metaverse.

2   'Screen Time Stats', *Exploding Topics*, https://explodingtopics.com/blog/screen-time-stats.

3   *'MrBeast to Launch First TV Series on Amazon Prime Video'*, Hollywood Reporter, January 12, 2024, https://www.hollywoodreporter.com/tv/tv-news/mr-beast-tv-series-amazon-youtube-1235854631/.

4   'YouTube's Dude Perfect Scores $100 Million-Plus Investment as It Plans New Texas HQ as "Family-Friendly" Entertainment Destination', *Variety*, 7 May, 2024, https://variety.com/2024/

digital/news/dude-perfect-100-million-plus-investment-texas-hq-1235965092/.

Epilogue

1   'Personal Update from Susan', *YouTube Blog*, 2023, https://blog. youtube/inside-youtube/a-personal-update-from-susan/

Scan QR code to access the
Penguin Random House India website